SWITCH DYN,

A practical approach to s'
medicines for self care.

C000201871

Anna Maxwell MRPharmS

Fizz Marketing Ltd
www.fizzmarketing.co.uk

SWITCH DYNAMICS
A practical approach to switching medicines for self care.

Copyright © 2013 Anna Maxwell MRPharmS

Anna Maxwell MRPharmS has asserted her right under the Copyright, Designs and Patents Act 1988 to be identified as the author of this work.

First published in 2013 by
Fizz Marketing Ltd.
Old Avenue Lodge , Old Avenue,
Weybridge, Surrey, KT13 0PS
United Kingdom

www.fizzmarketing.co.uk

Cover design & artwork by Joseph Pochodzaj
Author photograph by John Cassidy
Printed on acid-free paper from managed forests.
This book is printed on demand to order, so no copies will
be remaindered or pulped.

ISBN **978-0-9575372-0-0**

A CIP catalogue record for this book is available from the British Library.

We are grateful to the following copyright holders for permission to reproduce diagrams : Proprietary Association of Great Britain (PAGB), NHS Greenwich, Forest Laboratories, National Osteoporosis Society.

The author and publisher have made reasonable efforts to contact copyright holders for permission and apologise for any omissions or errors in the form of credits given. Corrections may be made to future printings.

INTRODUCTION

....

Why have I written this book?

I have spent over 25 years working in the pharmaceutical industry and am dedicated to helping people get better access to medicines for their own use, without having to go to the doctor for a prescription.

....

I registered as a pharmacist and in my early career as an Over The Counter (OTC) medicines buyer for Boots the Chemists, was part of the team that helped shape the health of the nation through the products and services sold by Boots. The team actively trawled global markets for products and services to bring to the UK to the benefit of the population and really make a difference to people's lives. Together we invented the concept of positive healthcare and released many prescribed brands from the depths of the dispensary to the wider world of self care. Latterly, as a marketing director I have worked with large and small multinational pharmaceutical organisations, presided over major innovation projects, created new self care categories, managed various switches (where a prescription medicine is transitioned to being available over the counter in a pharmacy) and worked with the government to create regulatory frameworks.

Innovation in the self care industry has been underwhelming, as has the relative level of investment in proven products for self care, when compared to the huge sums of money invested in biotech and telemedicine. I believe that there is significant untapped potential in the portfolios of drug companies that can be harnessed to create new medicines for the benefits of public health by transforming existing drugs into versions that can be bought over the counter. The problem is that people in drug companies generally don't know about this potential or how to release it. As a switch navigator I help holders of marketing authorisations successfully locate and mine the opportunities within their portfolios and bring them to market in the fastest time frame, at the same time avoiding the most common mistakes in their commercialisation and equipping them for the best chance of success.

Everyone wants to create the perfect switch, yet over the years I have noticed that typical mistakes get made over and over again. The industry works in silos; each company works on its own switches with no cross-fertilisation of ideas or shared learning and so the industry never moves on. Inventors learn from producing prototypes and repetition but there is not enough of this; as a result, there is limited experience to draw on and limited corporate memory. At the current rate of just over one switch per year, evolution in switch and medicines for self care is going to be very slow. I have watched over 30 switches develop and have worked on around a dozen.

What is this book about?

This book is about switch. In simple terms, switch is when a medicine that is under the control of a doctor is transitioned into a medicine that can be bought from a pharmacy or a grocery store through a combination of legal and marketing initiatives.

The recent handful of switches in the UK to date have not been particularly successful in financial terms, which is why the industry must improve its approach on a number of levels. It is time for a change, the world needs to get serious about switch and the people involved in switch at whatever level need to be enabled to get it right.

This book provides an information bank on what has gone before, identifying some of the pitfalls of switch based on practical, real- life experience. It also suggests a framework for running switch projects from concept to infinity and beyond.

Who is this book for?

1. Those working on a switch or thinking about it
2. Those who are tasked with delivering growth and innovation in healthcare companies
3. Intrapreneurs in healthcare organisations – those amazing individuals who just get things done
4. Government officials
5. Pharmaceutical entrepreneurs
6. Pharmacists and the pharmacy Press
7. People working on Rx brands in pharmaceutical companies
8. Marketing, communications and sales agencies who support the switch process in any way
9. Advocates of self care

"I believe that there is significant untapped potential in the portfolios of drug companies that can be harnessed to create new medicines for the benefits of public health by transforming existing drugs into versions that can be bought over the counter."

Anna Maxwell

Contents

How to use this book

Recognising that we all have busy schedules, Joe Pochodzaj has designed this book so it can be read at speed in less than an hour. It is a mix of case studies, practical advice and my take on switching medicines. You may agree or disagree with it and that's fine. It is a book of two halves: -

Chapters 1 to 5 bring switch to life in practical terms and use case studies to demonstrate some of the learning I have experienced.

Chapters 6 to 10 are for those of you who are planning a switch project and gives practical advice on what you need to do first, what to look out for and how to go about setting up your switch project for success.

Chapter 11 contains more case studies with my assessment of critical success factors. There are more examples to be found at www.dynamicswitch.co.uk.

Each chapter has a summary of contents at the beginning and I have also pulled together the key learning for clarity here too. If you want more detail, then read the chapter in full; otherwise, skip to the next section. It is up to you to grab what you need to become better equipped in your knowledge about switching medicines, what's involved and what you need to do.

Please enjoy the read and do write to me with any questions at anna@dynamicswitch.co.uk

Anna Maxwell

"In simple terms, Switch is when a medicine that is under the control of a doctor is transitioned into a medicine that can be bought from a pharmacy or a grocery store through a combination of legal and marketing initiatives."

Anna Maxwell

Chapter 1

ABOUT SWITCH

This chapter gives an overview of switch and why it is important to help reshape healthcare systems globally. It touches upon some of the challenges that have to be navigated in the process of switching a medicine from one level of classification to another.

7 FACTS ABOUT SWITCH

1. "Switch" is the process whereby a medicine is transitioned from prescription to a non-prescription status so that it can be made more widely available and can be bought by the general public in a pharmacy or a supermarket.

2. Switch empowers those people to take a more active role in maintaining their health without having always to refer to their doctor.

3. Switch aimed at treating common symptoms or preventing lifestyle-related disease can have a long-term impact on reducing healthcare costs for governments.

4. Switch enables untapped potential in the portfolios of drug companies to be harnessed as a source of innovation and portfolio development.

5. Switch can only work if pharmacists and doctors are on side so, as they are both very important drivers of the switch process, you have to learn what makes them tick.

6. Switch involves turning patients into consumers - a process that can take quite a while.

7. It is often said that most of the easy switches have been done and there are only complex ones left, but I believe that there are many possibilities still available.

"Switch involves turning patients into consumers." Once a switch has been implemented, people who ordinarily would seek advice from their doctor about their symptoms now have the choice to self-medicate and, in some cases, self-select."

WHAT IS A SWITCH?

"Switch" is the process whereby the legal classification of a medicine is changed from one level to another. This involves the demonstration of adequate risk benefit and safety criteria by negotiation with the relevant regulatory authority and stakeholders.

The regulatory process is usually brought about by the holder of a Marketing Authorisation (MA) and involves a pathway with distinct steps, channels and gates that have to be navigated, some in series and some in parallel.

Applications have to be justified with a clear rationale and backed by scientific opinion. It is prudent to engage stakeholders with the thinking in the early stages as their opinions are valued as part of the process.

The more challenging aspect of a switch is the process that converts patients into consumers. Once a switch has been implemented, people who ordinarily would seek advice from their doctor about their symptoms now have the choice to self-medicate and, in some cases, self-select. That is quite a shift in behaviour because it involves education, support and empowerment: factors that cannot be delivered in a 30-second television commercial.

Successful switch is about identifying a population that would benefit from that particular medication, then building a compelling proposition from grass roots up. This involves nurturing and managing the stakeholders, making them aware that self-medication is a possibility in their case, initiating a conversation about their specific situation, understanding their needs and reservations, forging a relationship then supporting them on a journey over time. It is most definitely not a quick fix!

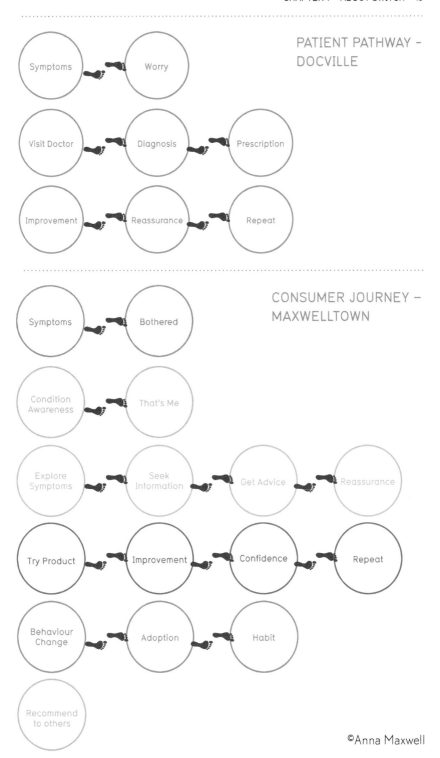

PATIENT PATHWAY -
DOCVILLE

CONSUMER JOURNEY –
MAXWELLTOWN

©Anna Maxwell

COUNTRY-SPECIFIC RULES

The legal classification of medicines varies from country to country, which in turn impacts their route of sale. For example, in the USA there are only two categories of medicine: Rx (prescription only) and OTC (Over the Counter). In the USA, switch is also referred to as Rx to OTC.

Within the European Union (EU) there are 27 countries, each with their own country-specific medicine legislation. Operating under a collaborative procedure for switch, the European Switch procedure is broadly based on the UK process.

Choosing a centralised European regulatory route is not always the best option, however, because of the varying attitudes of different member states to self-medication and switching medicines. This lack of agreement can result in lengthy debate and sometimes conflicting opinion, with the result that in most cases it is hard to get consensus.

European Centralised Reclassification process

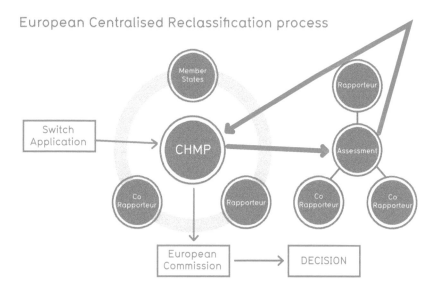

Under the centralised procedure there are nominated rapporteur countries and co-rapporteur countries. The switch proposal is submitted to the Committee for Medicinal Products for Human Use (CHMP) then first considered by rapporteur and co-rapporteur country(ies) and then by CHMP, which comprises members from all member states plus Norway, and Iceland.

Eventually CHMP gives an opinion that is then communicated to the European Union (EU) Commission which, in turn, makes the decision to grant or refuse the marketing authorisation. In 2008[1] GSK successfully achieved the first pan-European switch with Orlistat (Alli) in 27 European countries, a process that took many years to achieve.

Although the rewards from a pan-European licence position are potentially greater, the risks in pursuing a centralised routing are high. There is a huge amount of work involved, all of which soaks up available resources, it is certainly not a quick fix and success is not guaranteed.

In the last five years there have only been two approved centralised switches, Orlistat and pantoprazole. In the same time frame, there have been two withdrawals, sildenafil and ibuprofen/diphenhydramine hydrochloride combination, and one negative opinion, sumatriptan.[28]

It is rumoured that Pfizer was unable to persuade some countries of the benefits of OTC Viagra (sildenafil) on moral grounds, resulting in a pan-European rejection. More surprisingly perhaps, Galpharm's attempt to switch Sumatriptan (a drug for treating migraine) has been refused twice by the European Commission, even though the drug has already been switched in three European countries (UK, Germany and Sweden) and also in New Zealand. The concerns of the CHMP related to the safety of Sumatriptan Galpharm with respect to cerebrovascular and cardiovascular side effects, and in particular the potential for misuse and over-use. Despite the fact that non-prescription medicines for migraine are already available in many countries and have been for many years, CHMP also expressed concern about the risk of misdiagnosis of migraine and lack of medical follow-up when used in the non-prescription setting[29].

It is very difficult for a member state within Europe to break ranks and switch a product after the European Commission has made a decision to reject it. However, there is dissent: it is no secret, for example, that the UK authority, MHRA, is sympathetic to the switch of erectile dysfunction drugs because of the benefits in engaging men in primary care years earlier than they would normally present for related cardio-vascular conditions. A successful switch would also help combat the serious consequences of internet-supplied counterfeits.

"With a centralised route there is currently no mechanism for products that have been granted a Centralised Marketing Authorisation to switch on a local basis. That means that if the drug has been granted a centralised MA then at the moment the only route to switch is on a pan- European basis. Companies cannot switch one country at a time i.e. the switch has to mirror the centralised MA."

The UK MHRA is highly supportive of switch and has streamlined their process[23] to enable switches to be managed swiftly and efficiently. As a result, I would estimate that a switch could be delivered in the UK two years quicker than via the centralised European route.

One problem, however, with a centralised route is that there is currently no mechanism for products that have been granted a Centralised Marketing Authorisation to switch on a local basis. That means that if the drug has been granted a centralised MA then at the moment the only route to switch is on a pan- European basis. Companies cannot switch one country at a time i.e. the switch has to mirror the centralised MA.

This seriously threatens the feasibility and viability of some future potential blockbuster switches. One way of resolving this could be to enable member states to use the centralised MA as a reference product to switch in a particular country in the same way that generic medicines can use a reference centralised marketing authorisation to launch on a pan-European basis or in just one market. Another option could be where member states in the centralised procedure are sympathetic to switching medicines, then a change to non-prescription status is allowed in those countries for a period of time so as to gather real-life data.

One thing is certain, though: this roadblock for newer drugs with a Marketing Authorisation created in the centralised procedure needs to be sorted out fast if the government vision for self care is to be realised.

The alternative process for switch on a pan-European basis is to use a Decentralised Process (DCP) and or a Mutual Recognition Process (MRP)[30], neither of which tend to be very successful. Companies submit multiple applications in parallel grouped according to the attitude of the country clusters towards non-prescription medicine[28]; one set of applications in favourable switch countries and other set in the less favourable countries. In this scenario there is a designated Reference Member State (RMS) and Concerned Member States (CMS) and again a consensus is required in order to gain a positive opinion.

DUPLICATION – PARALLEL SUBMISSIONS MADE DEPENDENT UPON ATTITUDES TO SELF-MEDICATION

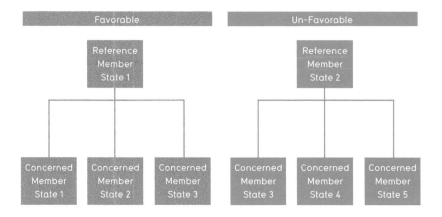

It is not hard to see why switches become challenging. Very quickly, even a decentralised switch can become a quagmire that soaks up resources, as well as being time-consuming and expensive to sort out because of the bureaucracy, politics and duplication involved to make it happen. In my view attempting to switch a medicine on a pan-European level is a difficult brief – by trying to suit every one, the process becomes knotted and overcomplicated, there are lots of hazards and it all takes far too long.

"In my view attempting to switch a medicine on a pan-European level is a difficult brief – by trying to suit every one, the process becomes knotted and overcomplicated, there are lots of hazards and it all takes far too long."

MEDICINE CLASSES

In the UK there are three classes of medicine relevant to switch: -

UK Medicine Classes		
POM	Prescription Only Medicine	Can be supplied on a doctor's prescription, under a patient group direction (PGD) and by some suitably trained independent prescribers
P	Pharmacy Only Medicine	May only be sold through registered pharmacy outlets under the supervision of a pharmacist
GSL	General Sales List	Can be sold from any outlet and from self selection without supervision

As the UK is in Europe, in some cases there is a blurring of legislation at the European level around food and cosmetics, which means that Food Supplement and Cosmetics regulations can also be relevant, dependent upon desired claims and labelling. For example, Vitamin D3 exists in a spectrum of formats and strengths as POM, P and food supplement. Certainly in the case of excipients, flavours and colourings and packaging for medicines, the MHRA is more widely adopting European Food Safety Agency Guidelines so there is a crossover between the legislative frameworks.

The most common UK switch routes are POM to P (prescription only medicine to pharmacy medicine, eg Diclofenac (Voltarol Paineze tablets) and P to GSL (pharmacy medicine to general sales list medicine), eg Diclofenac (Voltarol Emugel), Loratadine (Claritin). Other possibilities for switch also exist, taking them out of the medicines' legislative framework altogether.

Another type of switch - simple to undertake without reference to the medicines authority - is when a product is moved from licensed to unlicensed status. This has the benefit of saving the costs of managing and keeping updated the marketing authorisation which companies are obliged to do. The down side, however, is that the strength of the claims are weakened and marketing becomes more challenging. Examples of this type of switch are GSL to food supplement (certain vitamins), GSL to Cosmetic (mouthwashes etc) and GSL to medical device (skin barrier creams).

WHO NEEDS SWITCH?

If the problem of over-burdened healthcare systems is to be addressed, people also need to be empowered and enabled to prevent known lifestyle-related conditions and treat a range of other conditions themselves. Part of this is being educated to value good health and mobility in the first place and not to take good health for granted. In the US and Europe the population is ageing and with that shift in demographics comes not only additional expense for welfare and related systems but also the increased prevalence in age-related conditions.

In the UK the average cost to visit the GP is £25, the cost to visit a Walk In Centre £63 and a visit to A&E £59 to £117. [31] Yet the general public perceives NHS services to be "free". Overlooking these costs is a deep-rooted marketing problem that needs to be addressed. It is a cultural issue. Regardless of the promises the politicians make about maintaining funding in the NHS, the economic impact of the ageing population and UK demographic shift mean that in the future there will simply be not enough healthcare resources to go around and tough choices we have to be made for healthcare service provision in the UK.

"People need switch to give them better access to medicines without the need always to refer to the doctor...especially when the symptoms are easily identifiable or where they have encountered the condition before."

Being able to access medication at a pharmacy or grocer is more convenient and helps them get on with their lives with the minimum disruption, as well as creating independence around health.

Whilst writing this book I have spoken to many people who ask why they are unable to buy their child's Epipen, the Pill, Viagra, gout tablets, and anti-malarials etc direct from the pharmacy.

"Like it or not, healthcare professionals must acknowledge that there is a cohort of sensible people who are prepared to buy their medication and treatment for their own convenience and maintenance. ."

People also need to be given the opportunity to maintain their own health and the ability to prevent modern lifestyle-related conditions through a wider choice of products and services. In many diseases where prevention of risk would be of benefit, suitable medicines are not yet available over the counter and they are still in the domain of the doctor. Carefully thought through switch will enable this to change.

Osteoporosis, for example, is preventable. Bone mass in females starts to decline between the ages of 30 and 35 - something that most women are unaware of. So if governments could encourage people to look after their bones earlier in life and prevent the onset of osteoporosis through simple affordable measures (eg, a weekly preventive treatment for the price of a Starbucks coffee), then there will be more resources available to offer care for the other conditions that they and their families may experience in later life.

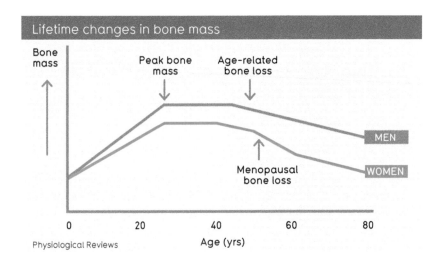

Lifetime changes in bone mass. (From Compston JE. Osteoporosis, Corticosteroids and Inflammatory Bowel Disease. Aliment Pharmacol Ther 9: 237-250, 1995)

"If governments could encourage people to look after their bones earlier in life and prevent the onset of osteoporosis through simple affordable measures (eg, a weekly preventive treatment for the price of a Starbucks coffee), then there will be more resources available to offer care for the other conditions that they and their families may experience in later life."

Rather than making one sweeping change I believe that a collection of smaller initiatives implemented by members of the public over time can reduce the pain and discomfort of the future inevitable changes. The sooner we as individuals make these choices the better. For example, enhanced communication by the NHS of the economics associated with your own personal use of it, might instil a mindset in you that is appreciative of the value and engender a "use sparingly" approach. In its Choose Well Campaign, NHS North West[31] makes users aware of costs associated with primary care visits and encourages people to visit NHS Choices website and their local pharmacy first.

"Asking the UK population to think twice before booking a doctor's appointment and visit the pharmacy instead as a first step in the road to their own recovery, could revolutionise the self-treatment market."

It could also increase the contribution that pharmacy can make in primary care and empower people to look after themselves a bit more than they do now.

Research has shown that NHS Choices, a high-quality information website that empowers individuals for health, saves the NHS £94 million a year in reduced GP consultations, proving it to be a popular and effective decision support tool permitting more efficient self-management and self-triage by the public themselves.

Combined with increasing access to information, self-triage and decision support tools online, switching some medicines from prescription to non-prescription status could make another contribution in bringing about a reduction in the NHS footprint. This would be achieved by enabling new medicines and healthcare services to be available that address the minor conditions and face up to major disease trends that people are experiencing this century.

Pharmacists and the pharmacy profession also need switches to create new self-medication possibilities, enhance the role of the pharmacist, provide better products and build the market. Switches serve as a mechanism to enhance and support the services that they provide on a walk-in basis. This, in turn, enables them to have regular opportunities to engage with consumers and give advice on medicines in which they are trained as experts.

However, there is a change required in the mindset of UK pharmacists that needs to be addressed regarding self- medication. Because some pharmacists think that it is cheaper for the person to get a prescription, they play a role in pushing people into GP's waiting rooms. This may be cheaper for the individual but it is not cheaper for the NHS. People who want to self- medicate – the time poor, cash enabled - should be empowered to do so as it is a virtuous choice.

Consultants, doctors and dentists need switch because they are at the front line in encouraging their patients to take greater responsibility for their own health. Switch can be deployed in prevention of disease; it can free up resources and enhance the value of the services they already provide. Switch can enable screening and early intervention to be done in the community with the first treatment step included as part of the regime before referral, thus allowing doctors to focus on more serious cases.

Healthcare professionals such as nurses, physiotherapists and podiatrists need switch because it empowers them to add a further level of care within the populations that they deal with.

The OTC industry needs switch to release the hidden potential in the drug portfolios of pharmaceutical companies, open up new self care possibilities, fill up the innovation pipeline for self- medication and nourish the Rx to OTC continuum.

Pharmaceutical companies deploy switch as a useful source of innovation it is a good way of using their molecules where possible in a different way for an additional target population i.e. the self-treater or preventer. It can extend the value of their existing assets and provide growth. Investment in new OTC medicines is limited; Pharma R&D investment is focused on serious disease biotech and personalised medicine and use of emerging technology. Many of the drugs available for OTC are over 50 years old, yet in food and cosmetics there are regular breakthroughs with new ingredients.

In the UK there are now more medicine purchases made from supermarkets than sold via pharmacy. In the last 20 years medicines have followed their course from POM to P to GSL but the innovation pipeline has not filled up enough at the other end.

"It is concerning that as products move through the Rx to OTC continuum there are fewer chances for pharmacists to intervene in healthcare conversations with the millions who pass through their doors each day. It is in the pharmacy where face-to-face interactions can really happen between real people and when people are in real need."

Just like any other market, pharmacy needs new products to continue to meet the demands of customers. It is concerning that as products move through the Rx to OTC continuum there are fewer chances for pharmacists to intervene in healthcare conversations with the millions who pass through their doors each day. It is in the pharmacy where face-to-face interactions can really happen between real people and when people are in real need.

The internet, telemedicine and information kiosks can enhance consumer understanding and provide support where face-to-face advice interaction is not possible or desired, such as in the case of emotionally sensitive conditions. However, these useful tools cannot fully replace face-to-face communication.

Insurance companies and banks need switch because it is going to be more difficult in future to underwrite life insurance in support of those with lifestyle-related conditions such as obesity, smoking and alcohol-related disease. If people have the means to prevent conditions such as the onset of diabetes without referral to the doctor, then they should have access to the toolkit to be able to do this. Switch would enable this to happen. It is not just in the UK; switch has implications of global proportions.

Governments can consider switch to facilitate change in behaviour as part of public health programmes that empower people to value their own good health, to look after themselves better and prevent the onset of disease. Across the world, healthcare systems are at breaking point and governments are looking for new ways to reduce the burden of their healthcare bill. People are living longer, populations are ageing and as medical science evolves, procedures that were once complex and only viable for a few are now available to many.

WHY SWITCH?

One of the commercial driving drug forces behind switch is the desire to extend the lifetime asset value of an existing drug molecule by making it available to a new set of sufferers via the self care channel. There is a right of passage that the molecule has to follow in its journey from a closed channel (prescription) to an open channel (non-prescription), suitable for self care.

Harvesting an existing portfolio as an Rx brand owner is a useful way of producing innovation without the need for extensive research and development associated with bringing a new drug to market. It also utilises existing resources available within the company to create the new opportunity.

"Although there are no set guidelines for when a switch process can be initiated, a period of five years as a prescription medicine is a good guideline – so if companies plan early enough, dependent upon the time taken for the regulatory process, they can gain four to five years of exclusivity."

Another reason for switching is to drive additional critical mass in a consumer health portfolio and increase sales potential. If this is done as part of a portfolio strategy, investment can be amortised across the portfolio and investment diverted from other areas of the business as required.

Some companies seek to extend the life of the molecule before patent expiry and the onset of the generic period. While this may seem to be a really good idea, historically companies have left it too late, allowing themselves a very short time to establish the new self care version before competitors arrive on the scene.

Although there are no set guidelines for when a switch process can be initiated, a period of five years as a prescription medicine is a good guideline – so if companies plan early enough, dependent upon the time taken for the regulatory process, they can gain four to five years of exclusivity.

Perhaps there may be an attribute of a molecule that can be better exploited in the self care setting or is a known side effect that has been observed that have an OTC implication, an off label use that could be utilized, or a different strength or format. For example sedating histamines are now used as sleep aids in the self care environment.

SOME OBSTACLES

The switch take-off profile

Considering the continuum of a UK switch from prescription only to mass market and wide self-selection is like supersonic travel, with two take offs.

Take off 1. From the runway, where the control of supply is regulated and heavily influenced by the pharmacist where the expected rewards are modest. Take off 2. In the air at full power that usually involves further change in status to a general sales list status (GSL) and access to the wider distribution channels. Most switches have followed the path from prescription status through to general sale and mass-market distribution. Historically it has been in the mass market where the full potential of the switched molecule is realised.

Pharmacists

There is some consternation from pharmacists regarding the right of passage for switch from POM to P and then from P to GSL. Some are resistant in the initial runway phase because they think it is a slippery slope to self-selection and will result in further loss of their share of trade to the supermarkets.

Partly this is the industry's fault in that the pipe hasn't been filled up with innovation that has driven the Pharmacy category. New P products are few and far between and switches have trickled through at one or two a year; most recently these have been lacklustre in terms of business performance.

Perhaps if pharmacists accepted the switch process from POM to P and then from P to GSL as a continuum and the natural evolution of a molecule's lifecycle, they could be persuaded to have an interest in enabling a product to transition to GSL and in to the mass market. Maybe they can be better rewarded in some way during the transition , after all, GSL medicines are still sold extensively in pharmacies.

Finance People

In my experience, portfolio strategy is historically not how most companies' P&Ls work. This means that switch products are made to stand on their own very early in their life cycle which, dependent upon the complexity of switch, may be completely unrealistic in a short time frame. Switches either don't make the drawing board at all or get killed very quickly when sales don't begin to materialise according to plan.

Joined-up thinking

If you are a brand owner and own the Rx molecule then it is inevitable that when the patent expires the generic products will arrive and around 70% of turnover of the Rx brand will be lost overnight – "the patent cliff".

What tends to happen is that companies get locked into debate about whether the Rx business or the consumer business can do a better job in preserving the value of the asset and whether a marketing dollar is better spent on shoring the Rx business, developing other Rx asset or in developing the consumer business, which is perceived to be more risky.

Precious resources and considerable energy are spent trying to resolve the argument, which is a circular one. There are plenty of examples - Canesten, Buscopan, Levonelle and Flomax Relief - where the Rx business has been increased significantly as a result of the switch and the combined sales are much greater than the Rx business would have been in the post-generic phase. It is the enlightened company that considers these as one P&L and a further enlightened company that chooses to do both.

"This process is not something that happens overnight; rather it is an evolution of mindset in the people to whom the message is relevant. Sales build over time and products that become brands have to work hard to achieve success."

Anna Maxwell

Chapter 2

POISONED CHALICE

There are established switches such as ibuprofen, acyclovir, clotrimazole and loperamide that have made their way from prescription to mass market. Yet the most recent switches, for example orlistat and tamsulosin have not been commercially successful to date.

As a result, there is a shroud of fear and a low level of confidence in the ability of switch projects to deliver growth, with a "switches don't work", "doomed to fail", "all the easy ones have been done" mindset within some consumer healthcare companies. For some they are viewed as a poisoned chalice to be avoided on the career path at all costs.

People move around jobs and companies much more than they did 20 years ago and there is very little switch experience and capability around globally. As a result, every time a switch project is initiated the team involved are pretty much starting from scratch.

The case studies chosen in this chapter are designed to unpick some of the drivers of successful and not so successful switches to provide a base line of information that you and your team should know prior to embarking on a switch project. There are more Case Studies in Chapter 8 and at www.dynamicswitch.co.uk.

THE 17 TABLETS OF SWITCH WISDOM

Learning #1
Pharmacists can make or break a switch.

Learning #2
Switches evolve: it is not a quick fix.

Learning #3
Switches require innovation for future sustainability.

Learning #4
Competition may be a good thing.

Learning #5
Understand how the sales protocol impacts the actual behaviour of your target and the consumer experience.

Learning #6
Success may show up in a different place to where you expect to find it – adjust your field of view.

Learning #7
Don't forget about prescription sales.

Learning #8
The consumer journey is a transition over time.

Learning #9
Be sensitive to consumer behaviour and changing attitudes and optimise them in your thinking.

Learning #10
Think carefully about the language that is going to be used in connection with the product and category.

THE 17 TABLETS OF SWITCH WISDOM

Learning #11

Products evolve into brands through evolution
Seed,germinate, growth, nourish, harvest, recycle,
adapt.

Learning #12

Plan switches early in the Rx product lifecycle and find ways
to cut time to market.

Learning #13

Proactively manage stakeholders throughout the switch
process from the beginning through to post launch and not
just in the planning stages.

Learning #14

Doctor intervention disrupts the intended consumer pathway
for a switch and the development of sales in the OTC setting.

Learning #15

Don't expect too much in the early stages at launch. It is too
big a challenge to expect switch products to stand on their
own two feet quickly – a much longer-term view is needed.

Learning #16

Set aside a level of investment in the first three years win
or lose so that an expert team have enough time and
resources to figure out the commercial path to success for
a switch.

Learning #17

Some switches may fare better online and through
technology there may be ways of establishing
brands at much lower investment.

POISONED CHALICE?

To get started I have chosen a few case studies in this chapter which highlight some of the challenges that previous switches have encountered. Learning from these examples can be incorporated into your thinking when planning a switch.

CASE STUDY 1
Hydrocortisone Cream 1% (POM to P)

The switch of Hydrocortisone 1% Cream embodied by Hc45 was probably one of the first I became involved with. It had been something of a frustration for pharmacists that, when people presented with minor skin irritations from an obvious contact allergy, for example near their belly button, a referral had to be made to send the person off to the doctor for a prescription for a mild steroid cream. This represented a no-win situation, an increase in the length of time that the person had to suffer, the sheer inconvenience of that person having to wait for an appointment and an unnecessary GP visit that could have been spent on more worthwhile cases.

In many scenarios the customer would be sold something sub-optimal to tide them over whilst waiting for the doctor's appointment (if they had bothered to arrange one), thus undermining the pharmacist's role and at worst resulting in no sale to reflect the value of the advice given to the consumer.

When Hc45 came along there was a new market opportunity created because there was an obvious niche. Crookes Healthcare (now Reckitt Benckiser) did a great job in educating pharmacist and pharmacy assistants through the trade press and paper- based modules and ran training events up and down the country.

However, one of the unforeseen consequences was that when consumers requested the product following an advertising campaign, pharmacists became cautious about the drug. Rather than selling it to the consumer, pharmacists picked out all the negatives communicated as part of the pharmacy supply protocol package on contra-indications, warnings and side effects. This resulted in them engaging in sales prevention mode in order to "protect" the general public from "harmful" use for fear they were being inappropriately motivated to buy the product because of the advertising.

This situation limited sales, increased doctor referrals and led to dissatisfied contact allergy sufferers who were still packed off to the doctor for a prescription. Unfortunately, this has rather set the trend for subsequent switches and as switches get more complex, engaging the pharmacist is a challenging hurdle to overcome.

Learning #1: Pharmacists can make or break a switch.

CASE STUDY 2
Nicotine Gum 1991 (POM to P to GSL)
My thanks to Alison Williamson for her contribution to this Case Study

It is quite interesting to reflect upon how the smoking cessation market has evolved over 20 years into consumer sales of £122.4m^2 per annum in the UK. However, sales on NHS prescription are still double that of the OTC business.

Nicotine gum had an interesting prescribing history in that it was launched in the UK in 1981 and was not allowable for re-imbursement on the NHS because despite its POM licence, it was considered a borderline substance (not a medicinal product with true clinical or therapeutic value) and therefore only private prescriptions were allowed and there were no reimbursable NHS prescriptions.

In 1984 Nicotine Replacement Therapy (NRT) products were automatically added to the blacklist (a negative list of products not to be prescribed under the NHS that included OTC categories such as cough cold products, laxatives, certain mild pain-relief products and vitamins[3]). As newer products were introduced to the market they continued to be blacklisted and researchers and practitioners including Dr Chris Steele[4] and the Scientific Committee for Tobacco and Health[36] advocated strongly that NRT should be available on NHS prescription.

The white paper Smoking Kills[37] in 1998 really helped build the argument from a Health Policy perspective. The tipping point was the launch in 2000 of Bupropion (Zyban) which has a different mode of action to NRT. GSK lobbied the Department of Health for reimbursement for Zyban and was given it - difficult for the DH to resist with all the targets and health policies in place. However GSK wanted Zyban to compete exclusively in the Rx arena with reimbursement and Niquitin CQ (NRT) in the over the counter NRT arena without reimbursement.

Only Pharmacia (Nicorette) lobbied for re-imbursement for NRT emphasising there should be an equality of approach and that NRT had a wealth of evidence

"NRT created a new competitive market space, which, combined with time, pharmacy services and a government-backed public awareness campaign has delivered a paradigm shift and a significant change in behaviour that ultimately saves lives."

to show it was effective in helping smokers to stop smoking.

GSK argued that making NRT reimbursable would diminish the advertising budgets which were important in helping to drive smokers to seek help and Novartis held a neutral position.

Far from diminishing advertising budgets, the combination of the reimbursed prescription and OTC business enabled sustained investment in the category leading to a significant impact on reduction of the smoking habit in the UK. Eventually in 2001 brand owners and collaborators won the right for smoking cessation products to be reimbursed. There are still a staggering 6.5m prescriptions written for smoking cessation products with a value of £125m per annum cost to the NHS. Grossed up to retail prices circa £250m, the prescription market still accounts for 60% of the total and enlightened companies like Johnson & Johnson (J&J) manage the two channels under the same management structure so that the Rx business benefits the consumer channel.

Nicorette and the Nicotine Replacement Therapy Market provides a great case study of how switch has created a new competitive market space, which, combined with time, pharmacy services and a government- backed public awareness campaign has delivered a paradigm shift and a significant change in behaviour that ultimately saves lives. Who could have imagined in the mid-nineties that there would now, 20 years later, be a ban on cigarette advertising, punitive measures for packaging and laws changing to make public areas, watering holes and gathering points becoming smoke-free zones?

There are a couple more contributory factors to the success of the smoking cessation market in addition to the drivers mentioned above. Prior to the innovation of NRT there were two products, now discontinued: "Stoppers", a confectionery line and Nicobrevin capsules containing quinine, methyl valerate, camphor and eucalyptus oil. A stop smoking category already existed but it completely reinvented itself with the introduction of NRT and this re-invention has continued through the evolution of products, formats and services over time which have replaced the outdated technology.

There has always been more than one brand in the OTC market. Whilst Nicorette Gum launched OTC first in 1991, it was followed very quickly (within a year) by the OTC launch of three patch brands: Nicorette (Pharmacia), Nicotinell from Novartis and Nicabate from MSD. Whereas Nicotinell and Nicorette battled it out with above-the-line television advertising, MSD launched with a below-the-line support programme for Nicabate.

Sir Tim Berners Lee[5] had not at the time invented the Internet so this was a low-key, paper-based programme in an envelope that accompanied the product and if users signed up for it they got some follow-up mailings by post. This type of patient support programme should have appealed to pharmacists; however, the advertising support placed behind both Nicorette and Nicotinell won over pharmacists and soon Nicabate was in the doldrums.

GSK gained Nicabate when they bought Hoechst Marion Rousell's OTC portfolio and in 1998 relaunched under the brand name of NiQuitin CQ. CQ stands for Committed Quitters and this was a revamped support programme that accompanied the brand. This new entrant sparked fierce competition in the market and a raft of NPD launches around the same time also fuelled the category.

Although Nicorette had the dominant market leader position, interestingly at the time Nicotinell was number 2 and Niquitin CQ No. 3 and the brands fought a battle for market share. A conventional marketing mix of above-the-line advertising, PR, sustained pharmacy training and the emerging support programmes were applied to drive awareness of NRT. The team at GSK smartly negotiated sponsorship of a Formula 1 racing car just as cigarette advertising was banned, with Niquitin CQ, a medicine, replacing the heavy sponsorship previously delivered by a cigarette company.

Some years afterwards I asked the Head of Consumer Brands at GSK whether there was any evidence of the impact that could be attributed to the racing car sponsorship but I was told that GSK were never quite sure of its effectiveness because it was not that easy to isolate and measure its impact on the sales line. For me it was an intelligent play and I firmly believe that the racing car sponsorship created an awareness that helped shift the paradigm and public opinion.

One of the key drivers in the success of Niquitin CQ was the critical insight. For a long time, Niquitin CQ patch had been the underdog and frowned upon because it was a 24 hour patch vs Nicorette's 12 hour patch. You don't smoke while you are asleep so why would you want a 24 hour patch? Nicotine at night = bad.

After some time, GSK found a way around this hurdle and turned it into a positive. They realised that people who did use the 24 hour patch were far less likely to crave a cigarette when they woke up in the morning – obviously a key daily danger point in terms of losing your resolve to quit. So, GSK trained pharmacists to ask the 'killer question'. When people came in asking about NRT, pharmacists were trained to ask 'do you crave cigarettes first thing in the morning/when you wake up?' If the answer was yes (more often than not) then Niqutin 24 hr patch was the answer. It was so beautifully simple and made rational sense to the pharmacists and pharmacy assistants so it worked like a dream.

In 1999 the government introduced its first smoking-cessation service and since 2006 pharmacists have been able to get paid for providing a smoking cessation service. There is now a strong network of NHS stop smoking services across the UK, but in England the responsibility for public health will move to local authorities in 2013 and it remains to be seen if they will continue to commission these services.

The other important part of the success of these products is in the innovation pipeline that has evolved over the last 15 years which has been carefully planned by the brand owners involved. Following the patch launches, the Nicorette Inhalator was launched in 1997, followed by the Microtab in 1998.

Also in 1999, the 2mg gum was switched to GSL and made available for general sale, opening up new non-pharmacy channels for distribution like supermarkets and petrol stations so that NRT could be as widely accessible as cigarettes[7]. Since then, the nicotine patches have switched and there has been a proliferation of new NRT presentations, with gums, lozenges, patches, sub-lingual tablets, nasal spray, mouth spray and inhalator all catering for different consumer needs and personal preference.

In summary, the combined efforts of the three competing brands working in a market over time with the collective aim of helping people give up smoking combined with a steady stream of innovation has delivered success. Of course government policy and the realisation that stopping smoking contributes to the greatest health gain has been a huge helping hand. If there had been only one brand in the market plugging away it would have been a very hard slog and would have achieved nothing like the impact that has been delivered by these companies in competition.

Learning #2: Switches evolve: it is not a quick fix.
Learning #3: Switches require innovation for future sustainability.
Learning #4: Competition may be a good thing.

CASE STUDY 3
Hyoscine butyl bromide 1991/2002 (POM to P to GSL)

Hyoscine butyl bromide switched in 1991 but remained a semi-ethical brand until it was repositioned and re-launched around 2002 as Buscopan IBS Relief for Irritable Bowel Syndrome (IBS) and achieved GSL status, enabling self-selection. The interesting thing about the Buscopan IBS Relief launch was that it had a slow start. IBS is a very difficult condition to diagnose and is done so through the process of elimination. At the time of launching Buscopan IBS Relief some doctors did not even recognise the condition.

Even though the product was GSL and available for self-selection, sales protocol required that the consumer had to get a medical diagnosis from a doctor first and this point featured on the label and in the advertising and promotion of Buscopan IBS Relief. Access to prescription data at the time would have enabled a 360° view of the combined Rx and OTC sales. About two years after the launch of Buscopan IBS Relief, it became apparent that the Rx version of Buscopan was enjoying a meteoric rise in sales, coinciding with activity generated for the consumer brand. By combining the sales of the consumer product with the uplift in the prescription variant there was a very healthy picture – what had been thought lacklustre was actually a big success.

On reflection, the prescription sales uplift is an obvious consequence of the supply protocol. IBS was a relatively unknown condition at the time and consumers were required to do a lot of self-exploration to work out for themselves what their problem was likely to be (and still do). Once they have come to a conclusion that their condition may be IBS, when a trusted voice like Buscopan IBS Relief tells them to visit the doctor for a diagnosis first before taking the medicine, it is likely that a proportion of these relief seekers will do as suggested. But of course, visits to doctors inevitably lead to the writing of a prescription for the drug: this is part of the dependency cycle of the doctor-patient relationship. Writing prescriptions is what doctors intuitively do and is what is expected of them.

In this scenario, the doctor visit is a key step for the consumer in identifying, confirming and controlling their symptoms and an important part of the process. For anyone who knows about IBS, it is a debilitating condition and can be extremely painful with a sudden onset so it is important to learn how to manage it. In real life these people may get two, three or even more prescriptions in the early stages of the condition but over time they become more confident and aware that they can pick up the same medicine in the pharmacy or grocery store. They transition to do so because it is altogether more convenient. I believe that the consumer sales in switch evolve once the consumer becomes confident enough to buy the product and regularly use it and this may take a few years.

The frustrating point about the revelation that a consumer marketing platform is driving prescription sales, is that when things don't go according to plan, brand investment gets curtailed and marketers are challenged with doing more for less. If there is transparency and it is clear to everyone that the Rx business is flying at the expense of OTC sales then it may be easier to maintain and possibly increase the investment in the switch to the benefit of more consumers.

" visits to doctors inevitably lead to the writing of a prescription for the drug: this is part of the dependency cycle of the doctor-patient relationship. Writing prescriptions is what doctors intuitively do and is what is expected of them. "

Compared to 2002 things are different now. Technology enables almost real-time tracking of performance, while intelligence from the field, pharmacists and consumers can be gathered really quickly, cheaply and efficiently. It is wise to use econometric modelling[8] techniques through the launch phase to evaluate each part of the marketing mix in order to figure out what is working and what is not.

I think it is recognised that when considering performance of switch in the early stages, it is critical to look at what is happening in the consumer business and also on the prescription business and as well as the competition. There may also be indirect consequences of your switch and it is important to understand all these drivers.

Learning #5:   Understand how the sales protocol impacts the actual behaviour of your target and the consumer experience.

Learning #6:   Success may show up in a different place to where you expect to find it – adjust your field of view accordingly.

Learning #7:   Don't forget about prescription sales.

Learning #8:   The consumer journey is a transition over time.

CASE STUDY 4
Docusate Sodium 2007 (P to GSL)

In the case of Docusate Sodium (DulcoEase), innovating and building a new sub-category within the laxatives market is a strategic measure intended to disrupt a market dominated by one brand (Senokot) that religiously outspent the competition by at least 2 to 1 and enjoys category captaincy with the major retailers.

Any marketing budget needs to work hard and cultural shift in attitudes driven by the Sex in the City TV show series meant that the time had come where previously taboo subjects were becoming regularly discussed by women over a glass of wine or over lunch. This behavioural shift helped the brand punch above its weight versus its investment level and the competition.

Constipation is not a subject that people feel comfortable discussing, even though it affects approximately 14 million[9] of us in the UK so in a bid to change the paradigm, a TV commercial called City Girls[10] was developed, loosely modelled on the TV series. There were viral elements built in to the ad to make it travel by word of mouth and a language invented to make it permissible to talk about the condition and the product. There was an express call to action to "Pass it on", encouraging conversation.

The City Girls ad was a success and delivered significant uplifts in sales and market share when on air. But there was another dimension: the ad really polarised people and got them talking, and articles started to appear in the broadsheets commenting upon it[11]. Advertising was extended by word of mouth because it was something worth remarking on.

Building new categories takes time and a key learning from the market and advertising spend data was that the same investment level delivered almost twice as many sales in Year 2 compared to Year 1. Nothing had changed; the ad was the same, the distribution static and the investment level similar. One explanation for this is that in the first year the marketing had attracted early adopters to trial the product but had also primed a whole lot more to think about the possibility. These consumers were persuaded in year 2, similar uplifts were observed in year 3 again achieving a greater sales level from the same investment.

This forms the basis of good analogy for how I think products evolve and establish themselves over time like a crop; sow the seed of an idea, germinate it, grow, feed, harvest, recycle, adapt.

This process is not something that happens overnight; rather it is an evolution of mindset in the people to whom the message is relevant. Sales build over time and products that become brands have to work hard to achieve success.

Learning #9   Be sensitive to consumer behaviour and changing attitudes and optimise them in your thinking.

Learning #10   Think carefully about the language that is going to be used in connection with the product and category.

Learning #11   products evolve into brands through evolution. Seed, germinate, growth, nourish, harvest, recycle, adapt.

CASE STUDY 5
Tamsulosin Hydrochloride

The switch of tamsulosin was first in class. To achieve pharmacy-only status this switch required a delicate mix of precision and skill to balance the needs of the authorities, the Marketing Authorisation holder, pharmacists, key opinion leaders, doctors, medical advisory boards, those consumers experiencing symptoms *and* their partners. OTC marketers mostly work on acute conditions but this is an OTC project for a chronic condition and the OTC intervention can actually save lives, thus making it highly rewarding for those involved.

Tamsulosin is used for the symptomatic relief of Lower Urinary Tract Symptoms (LUTS) otherwise known as BPH (benign prostatic hyperplasia), where men over the age of 40 have to make regular trips to the loo. It is inconvenient and embarrassing and gets progressively worse, impacting quality of life with the regular interruptions in the night and day affecting the sufferer and their partner detrimentally. The condition is caused by the prostate getting larger with age and pressing on the urethra (the tube that carries urine from the bladder).

The problem is that most men think it is a sign of getting older and do nothing about it. They simply don't realise that there is a one a day treatment that can take away the symptoms. They leave the situation for years, allowing it to get progressively worse and then one day in their 70's find that they can't go to the loo at all and end up in a life-threatening situation and a Transurethral Resection of the Prostate (TURP) operation. According to NHS Choices, there are an estimated 40,000 TURPs operations in the UK each year, many of which could have been avoided.

The switch was built upon strong rationale, medical opinion, stakeholder management and careful planning. It took over four years to overcome sensitivities involved - not necessarily around the condition of Lower Urinary Tract Symptoms (LUTS) but around concerns regarding what else the symptoms might be. Keeping up motivation and morale for all the stakeholders was critical.

The pharmacy model was built upon a shared-care principle with pharmacist making an initial supply based upon symptoms and the doctor confirming the

"science, marketing, pharmacy education and practice, regulatory affairs, retailing, communications, consumer behaviour and public affairs to name but a few disciplines."

diagnosis. There has been a lot of criticism about this method but at the time (c.2005) that was the only way the authorities would entertain the thought of a change to the regulatory status. Sometimes you have to take a scenic route to get to where you are going and move on from there.

Achieving the OTC Marketing Authorisation for tamsulosin called upon a breadth of experience in science, marketing, pharmacy education and practice, regulatory affairs, retailing, communications, consumer behaviour and public affairs to name but a few disciplines. The team became experts in the subject of LUTS, working with leading opinion leaders in the field.

Research states that 1 in 4 men over the age of 40 suffer this condition and the UK has one of the lowest treatment ratios, with doctors neglecting to treat the condition to the extent that their colleagues in Europe do. The benefit of tamsulosin is that it works very quickly, so in a couple of weeks the medication will have a result. If you haven't got an enlarged prostate and the condition is caused by something else, then it won't work and further investigation is needed of the symptoms.

It is recognised that men are not very good at proactively looking after their health and dealing with their symptoms when they occur, so more additional benefits of switching tamsulosin were that it would raise awareness and normalise a common men's health issue. At the same time it would draw men into the healthcare system earlier than they would normally present, meaning that they could be checked out for other conditions.

The mission to "draw men into pharmacy" was never going to be an easy task because men don't visit pharmacy[33] routinely like women do. When Flomax Relief launched in 2010, to treat the symptoms of BPH, there did not seem to be much investment devoted to advanced pre-launch marketing activity to pre-condition the target audience "seeding". It went straight to TV with a 30 second commercial that rather stereotyped the target audience. In my experience pre-launch marketing through the written and spoken word is key to successful switches because it pre-conditions the mind of the sufferer to begin to recognise their own

"In my experience pre-launch marketing through the written and spoken word is key to successful switches because it pre-conditions the mind of the sufferer to begin to recognise their own symptoms "

symptoms but there is always a balance to be struck between generating interest and awareness of a condition when you don't own the Rx molecule and the OTC product solution is not yet available. With medicines you can't very well put people on a waiting list and take product pre-orders like a new iPhone as their particular symptoms may require immediate attention from a doctor. However, it is possible, through technology, to start seeding campaigns to build relationships, give information, maybe even an entry level product such as a food supplement or herbal and begin a long-term conversation with the target audience in advance.

Following the launch fanfare for Flomax Relief, it seemed that investment was curtailed after a few months, before the category had time to establish any roots, as the early counter sales failed to materialise on plan in the OTC setting. Also in the press stakeholders, who had previously been in support of the switch changed sides to the opposition and came out against it, defending the territory of the GP and undermining pharmacist confidence. It is a shame for men's health that this happened and that the business apparently lost confidence so quickly. I believe that companies should set aside a ring-fenced investment for any switch in the first three years, win or lose, and accept that the first steps to market are the road test phase where the commercial model gets figured out by an expert team dedicated to making it work.

The training won awards. It was designed to meet regulatory requirements and focussed on the first purchase and did not really extend to the commercial reality of the whole consumer journey. The repeat purchase cycle was very important in the mix and there was less emphasis on this, although in training it needed to be tackled just as well to set out a clear consumer pathway.

When planning switch, it is important to bear in mind that there is a difference between the regulatory need and commercial requirements to make it work in practice; I will deal with this later when I talk about protocols and pharmacist training. At launch, this disconnect may have caused confusion for pharmacists, naturally capitulating a default position of sending the consumer to the doctor, which is the easiest thing to do if you are in doubt.

'The Consultation Moment of Truth" (CMOT) – the first customer arrives

"Flomax Relief, now let me think...
I know it's in here somewhere!"

When tamsulosin went OTC, one Internet pharmacy business created a Flomax Relief online store within its website. Via an online screener, which was a consumerised version of the pharmacists' protocol and subsequent pharmacist consultation, a strong sales profile was built through search engine optimisation and pay per click. As a result, Flomax Relief quickly became a Top 10 seller.

The pharmacy worked very hard at building sales in the early stages and to get the sales and repeat process right. There was a personal intervention by phone between the pharmacist and consumer and great feedback.

Offline, in the bricks and mortar pharmacies, the pharmacy protocol was deemed too lengthy and pharmacists quickly lost interest in it. Rather than buy tamsulosin over the counter as intended, the first wave of consumers were mostly sent to or proactively visited the doctor in large numbers and were written prescriptions for generic tamsulosin instead.

The shared care model facilitates a doctor consultation and therefore it was fairly predictable that there would be uplift in prescription sales as a result of the OTC marketing efforts. Unfortunately, by the time the switch was finally approved, the Flomax patent had expired and generics picked up the sales rather than the parent brand.

The published data for Flomax Relief reads over the counter sales at a lacklustre £640,000[14] However, in 2011 there were 526,000 more prescriptions written for tamsulosin 400mcg than in the previous year, at a cost to the NHS of £2.0m.[15]

"the self care industry just haven't figured out quite how to commercialise the product in the OTC setting.".

Let us look at the combined picture and these results in another way against the objective of drawing men in to the healthcare system earlier to get their LUTS treated. It looks as though something has changed as a result of the switch of tamsulosin and the change was quite substantial in driving prescription business. I am fairly certain that if the 526,000 prescriptions had been OTC purchases, then Flomax Relief would have smashed its commercial targets way beyond expectations.

In summary, the problem with the Flomax Relief launch is that pharmacists and the self care industry just haven't figured out quite how to commercialise the product in the OTC setting. Tamsulosin has already earned its place as a blockbuster and will be hopefully around for a long time to help those with LUTS, save lives and deliver further return on investment for the company and the market place.

The big issue is that there is still a huge proportion of the male population suffering with LUTS symptoms. These people are still under-diagnosed and under-treated and perhaps some of them have more serious underlying conditions that need to be checked out. With little investment in the category the status quo will remain.

Time has moved on and there is a lot that can be learned from the marketing strategy of the Tena brand, who subsequently have set about building a related category in bladder weakness. They supply protective underwear (new language for incontinence pads) and have been hugely successful. This is great seeding activity for the brand owners of Over Active Bladder drugs such as Oxytrol (Watson Pharma), Vesicare (Astellas) and Detrusitol (Pfizer), who may decide to switch their molecules in the future.

Learning #12   Plan switches early in the Rx product lifecycle and find ways to cut time to market.

Learning #13   Proactively manage stakeholders throughout the switch process from the beginning through to post launch and not just in the planning stages.

Learning #14   Doctor intervention disrupts the intended consumer pathway for a switch and the development of sales in the OTC setting.

Learning #15   Don't expect too much in the early stages at launch. It is too big a challenge to expect switch products to stand on their own two feet quickly – a much longer-term view is needed.

Learning #16   Set aside a level of investment in the first three years, win or lose, so that an expert team have enough time and resources to figure out the commercial path to success for a switch.

Learning #17   Some switches may fare better online and through technology there may be ways of establishing brands at much lower investment.

SO WHAT?

This all raises a number of issues in category start-ups and switches. What is the right marketing mix? What is the appropriate level of investment? How can pharmacists be switched on? How much time should companies invest for? Do you need a big bang or a slow burn? What is the role of TV? How can technology improve performance of early-stage switches? Importance of the questionnaire and pharmacist intervention? How can doctors become facilitators of successful switch?

There are also some strategic questions too: how joined up is the consumer and pharmaceutical division in their thinking – do they even talk? Does the company have any interest in the prescription business at all? When is the right time to start planning a switch? Is it more commercially advantageous to own the Rx brand and the consumer product or go it alone? What have we overlooked?

17 SWITCH COMPLEXITIES

1. You get what you pitch for. Set yourself up to succeed and you will.
2. Put the consumer at the heart of your thinking.
3. Build the right team.
4. Pre-wire the product so that it works intuitively.
5. Crash test the strategy to destruction at every stage and make it better.
6. Make sure you engage with people who know about switching medicines.
7. Measures of success depend on the stakeholders concerned.
8. Use wider metrics than sales and return on investment to evaluate switches in the early stages.
9. Time is a critical success factor and is the most valuable metric.
10. Switch should be part of the design of the Rx product to extend a molecules lifecycle post patent expiry.
11. Pharmacist and HCP training should be built on a see one, do one, teach one methodology.
12. Think about how pharmacists could be remunerated for the time they spend counselling a potential switch consumer.
13. Annual budget allocations, payback methodology and budget cuts hinder switch planning and preparation.
14. Appropriate funding levels should be ring-fenced and protected for the duration of the project.
15. Don't allow your switch to get crushed in the "rush."
16. An innovation pipeline is a key part of any switch plan.
17. As a result of global thinking, niche switch opportunities in the UK are being overlooked.

Anna Maxwell

Chapter 3

WHY SWITCHES DON'T WORK

Like a quality timepiece, switch projects are intricate and require precision engineering. Success results from the design of the product, the people involved and the process. Every switch is unique, the process is dynamic and success is derived from combining hundreds of elements in a delicate balance.

The key question most people ask me is why have some recent switches failed? It is an interesting question because there is no clear-cut answer and in all the articles on the subject that I have read I don't think I have ever seen a comprehensive response, and this is one of the main drivers for me in writing this book. Usually there is only time to discuss one part of the story; some blame the regulations, some the sales protocol, some blame pharmacists or others blame the marketing or consumer demand there are a myriad reasons.

Every switch is unique and the switch process involves a journey that not only takes a product from one legal status to another but also takes the consumer through a transition of behaviour change and this takes time. In planning a switch there is a regulatory journey, a marketing journey and a consumer journey to be taken. There is no quick solution: the regulatory process may be a switch but the rest is a transition – a transformation of ideas and people's behaviour over time.

Here is my take on some of the current problems with Switch: –

MINDSET

All too often the thinking behind the switch is driven by replicating what happens in the prescription world rather than thinking about the behavioural aspects of the consumer in the self care setting. If switches were developed from the other end of the telescope , ie starting from the consumer perspective without the influence of drivers for the prescription business, then a switch will have far greater chance of success.

ASK THE RIGHT PEOPLE FROM THE START

Success needs to be built into the design of the product right from the outset: every aspect of who it is for, what it does, why and when they should use it. As far as possible, everything about it should be intuitive, so the name, packaging, label, key messages need to be well thought through, as this will facilitate eventual confident use of the product in the consumer setting.

The implications of this means that in the early stages of a switch, relevant stakeholders need to be involved to flush out the reasons why the switch won't work as well as the reasons why it will, so that these obstacles can be overcome in the design of the overall product and package. Pharmacists, doctors, pharmacy groups, consumers and influencers should all be engaged early during the development of the concept to build 20:20 foresight on the switch.

"Success needs to be built into the design of the product right from the outset"

SUCCESS MEASURES

Success measures for various stakeholders are very different. The regulator views success as achieving the reclassification itself, yet the pharmaceutical company is looking at commercial success in terms of return on investment. The Department of Health may view success in a number of ways, including number of patients being screened (azythomycin), number of men consulting about LUTS (tamsulosin), number of quitters (NRT).

Globalisation of marketing departments means companies seek the biggest opportunities to span the widest number of territories in order to deliver total world domination. This means that smaller niche opportunities in particular markets are overlooked in favour of the blockbusters because the numbers are apparently not there, yet there exists a sizeable prescription following for the niche switcher. I have seen the scenario time and time again where projects get canned because the numbers are too small – this is unfortunate for the UK population who are stuck with medicines developed over 50 years ago.

Sales targets have typically been the measure of success for pharmaceutical companies but such targets are generally borne out or forced by payback models to meet company expectations that for new categories have regularly proven to be unrealistic. If the category, for example hay fever, is already established and sizeable, then a three-year payback might be feasible. On the other hand, building a new category such as Over Active Bladder from scratch, the 5-10-year range is a far more appropriate expectation.

If early success measures were based on condition awareness, website hits and number of additional conversations occurring in the primary care setting on the category, prescription uplift etc; and investment levels were viewed as research and development not sales and profit; then switches would start to get somewhere.

TIME

Time is a critical success factor on a number of levels and is the most valuable metric. The chart below shows the work schedule associated with switch projects as they are typically managed.

WORKLOAD CHRONOLOGY OF A SWITCH PROJECT

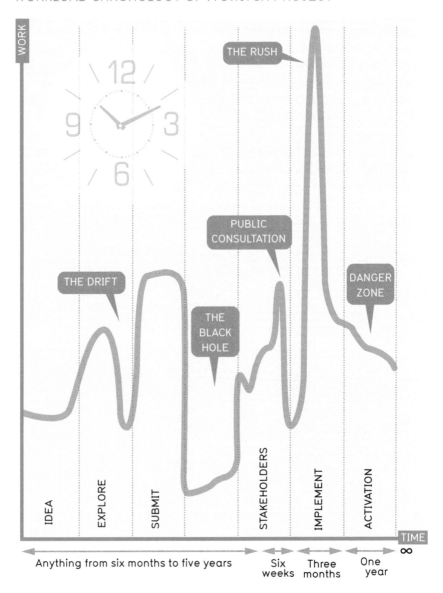

Time to start thinking Pharmaceutical companies do not think about switch as a natural evolution of a patented prescription drug's life cycle where a dip in profitability is accepted as a natural phenomenon of transitioning to the post patent phase and building an OTC business. Companies tend to wait until the generic period is looming when inevitably 70% of the patented business falls off a cliff overnight. Shortly before this happens (about three years, dependent upon business planning cycles) a battle commences about which division Rx or OTC can do a better job at plugging the sales gap – no one wins. A switch of a drug can be considered much earlier than that and is possible after approximately five years of patent life. If companies accept OTC as an inevitability and join up the thinking between the Rx division and the consumer division, the Rx business and the OTC business can develop a plan side by side, with the Rx business generating the investment during transitional period rather than the switch being expected to stand on its own two feet from day one.

Lost Time (The Drift) - companies are very good at generating lots of this in the switch process by not setting the switch up in a managed way with a team (which can be virtual), a critical path and key milestones. The steps involved in switch projects do not necessarily fit into the typical launch processes adopted by large and small organisations because the regulatory element is to a certain extent open-ended and out of the control of the company.

Switches can easily drift because they operate outside the usual system yet, just like any other project, switch projects need a mapped out process and timeline and, if set up this way, can be aligned to existing procedures. Switch projects do not have to take years to bring to market; the industry has sunk into bad habits. Speed up! There are lives to improve.

Too little time - I have regularly observed the scenario where a busy product manager is given a switch project to lead on top of an already heavy workload just because the category concerned just happens to fall under his or her own brand portfolio. Sometimes the Switch Torch is given to a new hire who has get to grips with a new role in a new company as well as the challenge of running and delivering a switch project. So it is no surprise when that individual is only able to devote one or two hours a week to the project, sandwiching it between their lunch break, meetings and run-of-the-mill presentations. This type of scenario is not fair on the individuals, as they are not being given the headspace to think around and plan the switch to deliver the best outcome for the benefit of pubic health. Such practice is to the detriment of the project that undoubtedly requires significantly more focus than the time an already busy person can allocate in their crushing schedule. Because the product manager is always fire-fighting and try-ing to learn at the same time, life becomes a vicious circle, things get overlooked, mistakes are made and the time to market just gets further and further away.

This is no way to run any project of significance. Switch projects need to be al-located time and, if set up correctly with the right team and aligned resources with an injection of experience, can be managed seamlessly to get the work done quickly and efficiently on top of the regular workload. Make switch Mission Criti-cal for everyone involved.

The black hole – this is the term I give to the period after submission of the documentation to the regulatory authority when the regulator makes their as-sessment. Government bodies have a reputation for taking time to ponder on matters but given there is a fee paid with the submission to pay for the time I be-lieve that it is perfectly justifiable for a regulatory team to manage the MHRA just like one would manage a conveyancing solicitor in a house purchase. For some reason, most likely driven by other corporate priorities, regulatory departments become fearful - unable to pick up the phone to the assessor and so play a waiting game rather than annoy them, thus delaying things further. This inevitably leads to delay because the assessors concentrate on their priorities, which are always something other than your switch. The black hole gets deeper…

The clock stop – this is the term given to the period after the regulatory body has given the initial response. It is another reason for unnecessary delay as teams scramble to get their act together following a request for information. The clock might stop but time doesn't and this can absorb many days. This period is sometimes viewed by some as a breathing space, a natural pause in proceed-ings, which it is not. Having to wait two to three weeks to get a team together for a meeting on the subject to plan the response is typical, so in most organisations weeks and months go by. Minimising delay has to be a priority for switch teams. Hurry up, there are people suffering out there!

THE RUSH

As a result of long and uncertain regulatory journey times and in some cases concerns about confidentiality, the way many companies approach switch projects is to submit an application to the regulatory authorities and wait until the marketing authorisation is definitely on its way. Budgets to cover launch preparations can be locked until the approval is on the horizon. In such circumstances, once the application is known to be approvable, the marketing team galvanises themselves to get the product to market as fast as they can. There is a lot to do and this creates a huge crescendo of work generally linked to the manufacturing lead-time, which is usually about three months. This is driven by the availability of the packaging components, which is usually the critical item as it is high risk to print them before the Marketing Authorisation has been approved.

If a big team is allocated to the project then it may be possible to pull the implementation off in that time frame but usually there are one maybe two brand managers allocated who then have to work round the clock 24/7 to get market ready and this puts massive pressure on everyone else too. There are a few problems with this approach:

i.   locked down budget pots mean than planning and preparation can't be done in advance in any detail.

ii. It doesn't allow enough time for advanced marketing of the switch, ie seeding generic and category messages in the press and online which is a crucial element of awareness- building prior to the launch.

iii. Larger customers who generally require more notice than three months have to be swept up in the process. They need to agree the listings, organise training, range reviews, shelf rebuilds and like to have input. Retailers complain they aren't given enough time and this impacts their motivation and enthusiasm for the switch.

So, potentially great work gets crushed in the rush.

EXPERIENCE

People move around in companies much faster than in the last decade and as a result only a fraction of the corporate memory about switch has been retained, with most approaching switch as a new initiative. Very few people running switch projects have actually worked on a switch from end to end so I have found that experience within organisations attempting switch can be very limited. Many smaller organisations and most switch teams I come across are approaching switch for the first time and the pressure on them is immense to get it right – this is a loaded challenge. Inventors evolve a series of prototypes and IT projects require beta tests and upgrades, why should a switch project be any different?

To help in these circumstances, an injection of resource from people who know about switches is beneficial to input into the design of the switch concept, the switch project and also to facilitate the process through their organisation and commercialise it. With so many variables for each switch, is it sound thinking to imagine that we will get each switch exactly right first time around? Managing expectations is really important.

RECOMMENDATION

Pharmacists are very good at referring consumers back to the doctor for a prescription. They think they are doing the consumer a favour because it is cheaper for them to get a prescription, yet this practice is undermining their business and

"only a fraction of the corporate memory about switch has been retained, with most approaching switch as a new initiative. Very few people running switch projects have actually worked on a switch from end to end"

position in primary care. It would be better if pharmacists could be encouraged to think more about the cost of a GP visit and prescription and how medicines bought in the pharmacy actually represent a saving - not only in terms of revenue for the public purse but also the convenience of time saved for the surgery and the consumer. There is a dilemma here though, as the cash profit made on the sale of an OTC switch probably does not cover the time involved in selling it. How does the pharmacist get remunerated?

The regular referral of potential self care consumers by pharmacists back to the surgery for minor ailments may be one of the reasons why the OTC market is not growing as quickly as pundits hoped. However, more fundamentally, over half of OTC sales actually occur from self-selection which means the number of conversations about healthcare are just not happening like they did in the 80s and 90s. This is not great news for pharmacy intervention. Yet a few successful switches that drive people to ask in pharmacy can reverse this trend because they can increase the number of healthcare conversations that occurs day to day. Of course, pharmacists should encourage healthcare conversations at every point of contact to educate consumers and change their perceptions around self care.

Pharmacists are in a great position to identify cohorts of people that might need a certain product or service and sell it to them over time but this has to come from a genuine interest in their health and wellbeing rather than a purely commercial gain. For example, a women in her 40s who arrives in the pharmacy with a plaster cast should be expressly recommended and sold a Calcium and Vitamin D supplement.

It is the case, however, that pharmacists and pharmacy staff are not trained in the art of selling. Counselling combined with selling skills need to be learned and honed to enable pharmacy to keep their customers healthy, happy and in control of their wellbeing.

SALES PROTOCOL

Imigran Recovery Migraine Questionnaire Questions 1 to 5 of 8.

Imigran Recovery Migraine Questionnaire

Please answer the questions below by ticking the boxes that apply to you.
If you are not sure about any of the questions, leave them blank and the pharmacist will help you.

About you...

	Yes	No
Are you under 18 years of age?	Yes	No
Are you over 65 years of age?	Yes	No
If you are female, are you pregnant, do you think you might be pregnant, or are you breast-feeding?	Yes	No
Have you had fewer than 5 migraines in the past?	Yes	No
Did you have your first ever migraine within the last year?	Yes	No

If you have answered 'Yes' to any of these, please speak to the pharmacist before going further.

About your migraines...

1 Has your doctor given you any medicines for migraine?	Yes	No
2 In the last three months, has a headache interfered with your activities on at least one day?	Yes	No
When you have a headache, do you feel nauseous (sick)?	Yes	No
When you have a headache, does light bother you?	Yes	No
3 Roughly how many migraine attacks do you have each month? *Attacks per month* ▶		
How long does the headache part of your migraine usually last (as opposed to other migraine symptoms) if you don't take any medicine, or if it doesn't work? *Hours* ▶		
How many days a month do you usually have a headache of any type (including a migraine headache)? *Days per month* ▶		
In between your migraine attacks, do all the symptoms of your migraine go away?	Yes	No
Do your migraines follow a broadly similar pattern each time?	Yes	No
4 When you have a migraine headache, do you get any other symptoms apart from nausea/sickness or sensitivity to light or sound? If yes, please write down these symptoms.	Yes	No
Other symptoms		
5 Did the symptoms of migraine occur for the first time over the age of 50?	Yes	No

Now turn over

If you want to buy Imigran Recovery again, simply bring this Treatment Card to your Pharmacy.

· Please read the Patient Information Leaflet before taking this product
· Please tell your doctor that you are taking this product
· Tell your pharmacist if your migraine has changed in any way
· For further information go to www.ImigranRecovery.com

IMIGRAN
RECOVERY
sumatriptan

I have completed the Migraine Questionnaire and my pharmacist has agreed I am suitable for Imigran Recovery.

Name of Customer _____

Date of Issue _____

© Forest Laboratories

A number of the more recent switches have been accompanied by a questionnaire (sales protocol) that has unfortunately led to consumers being interrogated by pharmacists at the point of consultation. In some cases they are actually used as a sales prevention tool rather than a bridge between pharmacist and consumer to create a suitable sale and a satisfied self care customer.

Unwieldy sales protocols are not liked by pharmacists and there is support to move away from these in favour of greater signposting on the labelling, continuing professional development and a few counselling questions...easy in theory, not so easy to achieve in practice with more complex switches.

It is fair to say that questionnaires have become a kind of contract between the brand owner and regulator as a standard operating procedure by which pharmacists would screen patients for their suitability for a particular medicine and for their protection. It is like a constitution between both parties or a framework acting in the interests of consumer safety; yet the pharmacist has not bought in to this approach.

"if people are actually bothered enough to ask about a particular medicine or condition then they have probably done some homework and are already quite informed"

For more complex switches I do think that some form of framework is useful because the process distils the decision tree into the few salient points that matter to the consumer and the safe use of the product. It is important to draw out any red flag symptoms in the process. It is bizarre that in physiotherapy, complementary medicine and private healthcare a half-hour consultation has come to be expected, but in the case of pharmacy we apparently want to get the consumer out of the door as quickly as possible. I guess the difference is that the pharmacist counter consultation is unpaid, but what if there was a mechanism to generate a fee for a 10-minute pharmacy consultation?

As a communication tool, such assessment consultations could be turned into positive, educational experiences for the consumer and if the process is reverse engineered - perhaps with the questionnaire being completed by the consumer, as part of the rite of passage - the process could be even more engaging for them.

In my experience, if people are actually bothered enough to ask about a particular medicine or condition then they have probably done some homework and are already quite informed. The Internet makes this even more possible, so the very fact that they present and have bothered to seek advice almost makes them eligible for supply.

I have not observed consumerised questionnaires being employed with any weight in the marketing of switches. A lot of this is down to the fact that there has been to date, no effective way to distribute them through pharmacy, and consumer magazines would rather fill their pages with advertisements. New technology provides an opportunity here for the information seekers and explorers.

WWHAM (see glossary: a mnemonic for assessing symptoms in pharmacy)

As a pharmacist I have never viewed the questionnaire accompanying switched products as anything other than an aide memoire to act as a prompt for the pharmacist until they learn it and the process becomes intuitive for them. It is just a WWHAM process for a new product but if you are only seeing one customer a week (if that), the reality for most pharmacists with recent switches, then it takes a long time to get up to speed and for the process to bite and become intuitive. In that scenario and when under pressure, sending the person to the doctor is the line of least resistance and I have seen it happen many times.

INTUITIVE TRAINING

The problem is that up until now there has been no way to reach all pharmacists consistently to get them up to speed on new products quickly. Sales forces in the main only call on the top 3500 independents and the multiples have procedures regarding their training programmes, which determine the way in which it is delivered and there is very limited face-to-face contact.

What happens is that various methods of training and communication are employed, usually via the trade press, to communicate switches. As a result, it is disparate and done amongst the clutter of everything else so the messages get diluted. It is not unusual for four different flyers to fall out of trade publications at once, on four different brands, with a whole host of messages and when you are trying to promote the key rationale for a switch this is not an ideal way to get your message across to encourage a new behaviour in a pharmacist!

Doctors are trained with a process of see one, do one teach one, which really works but getting even an hour of face time with a pharmacist to train them on a new product is really tough. Some companies have run one-off road shows or seminar evenings but the style of these are usually "tell" rather than role play and practise and only a tiny fraction of the pharmacist universe is reached through this method - it is an expensive way of doing it.

In the 80s, Janssen (J&J), preferring not to spend their money on above-the-line advertising, built a business initially by using their pharmaceutical representatives to visit pharmacies in the afternoons. In 1985 they invested in a detailing force that called upon independent pharmacy training and educating pharmacists and pharmacy assistants. They also had products that were first in class; efficacious and targeted against specific niche brands such as Imodium, Daktarin, Stugeron and Vermox. All these were groundbreaking switches that have been sustained.

For more complex switches, I would like to see the type of detailing in pharmacy that helps change behaviour of pharmacists to embrace switches and also forges a link between doctor's surgery and the pharmacy at the community level to make the switch work for everyone. In reality, for most companies this means closer collaboration between pharmacy-facing representatives and doctor-facing representatives in the field.

Make it happen!

I think it would be a good idea for pharmaceutical companies to approach early-stage switch as research and development projects with the aim of finding the right way to commercialise the molecule in the self care setting.

There should be a guaranteed investment level for this period, win or lose.

Anna Maxwell

Chapter 4

MAKING SWITCHES WORK

This chapter covers my thoughts on what needs to change in the way switch projects are handled from the outset based on my practical experience of running and implementing switch projects.

11 NEW SWITCH DYNAMICS

1. Consider the initial stages of switch as R&D to find a way to commercialise the product in the OTC setting.
2. Ring-fence the funds required to undertake the switch, win or lose.
3. Make sure that people have the time and resources to do it properly.
4. Invest in people who know about switch as part of your process.
5. Get the right heads in the room at the right time.
6. Keep it simple.
7. Plan well, be flexible: it is a dynamic process.
8. Understand the consumer mindset and journey.
9. Harness the power of emerging technology.
10. Know where the hurdles are build 20:20 foresight.
11. Think about the game changers.

MAKING SWITCHES WORK

It is time for change in the way companies approach switch projects. In the future it would make sense if, where possible, self care attributes were designed into the prescription product and it was assumed at the outset that the natural pathway for the drug is to undergo a period of time under doctor supervision, then pharmacist supervision before being released into the self care arena in some form. However, I recognise that this will take a couple of generations to achieve and is a long-term vision.

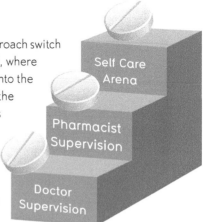

SET THE SWITCH PROJECT UP AS R&D

We are where we are, so in the meantime I think it would be a good idea for pharmaceutical companies to approach early-stage switch as research and development projects with the aim of finding the right way to commercialise the molecule in the self care setting. The initial objectives of any switch project should be to establish whether it can be sold in the self care setting and to find a way to make the sales method scalable.

I think that new metrics are needed to evaluate switches in the early stages and over time. Perhaps the first three years in the life of a switch would be better considered as a test and trial phase where the product, brand, communications, consumers and influencers are under constant review. The future success relies upon establishing the mechanism and the process that will deliver volume uptake and sustainability of a new medicine, either for treatment or prevention. There should be a guaranteed investment level for this period, win or lose.

Being realistic, there are conversations that do need to take place about return on investment with the finance directors so in my experience there are probably two scenarios that can be employed at the outset, each with its own payback criteria:-

Established category - If the market is already established, eg allergy, and your molecule offers a significant differential over the existing OTC offer, then it is reasonable to expect a return on investment over a three-year period and a conventional product launch P&L evolution.

New category - If your challenge is to invent a new self care category, then this involves taking patients, pharmacists and other healthcare professionals on a journey from doctor-led to proactive self care. This takes time and so payback using traditional marketing models will be much longer - more like 7-10 years.

"Switch requires an investment of time up front in the strategic development phases and specific expertise from people who know about switch. People need to be given the time to do it properly."

INVEST TIME , BUILD MOMENTUM

Every switch is unique and more complicated than a regular piece of new product development. Switches do not quite fit into the regular new product planning processes typically used by pharmaceutical companies, so they can quickly become derailed. With careful planning it is possible to align them to internal processes and it is advisable to hire a switch navigator to design your switch programmes to integrate with your company process and to help your company commercialise it. A momentum for switch needs to be built and the project infused through the organisation with the tenacity of a virus.

Switches require the best brains to think through the positioning, regulatory strategy and implications within the self care setting for each market considered and that means harnessing the expertise that exists within the company up front and getting the right heads in the room in the very very early stages. The people involved need to know who they are and what is expected of them.

WORK OUT THE CONSUMER JOURNEY

Work out and understand the human behaviour at every stage of the sales process including the roles that pharmacists and other healthcare professionals will play.

HARNESS THE POWER OF EMERGING TECHNOLOGY

New technology provides possibilities for brand owners with innovative switches to connect with people in a far more intimate way and at much lower cost than ever before. Through the use of carefully thought through websites, apps, social and digital marketing campaigns, brands are now able to foster a deeper engagement with self care consumers. Consumers can even do some of the self-assessment work themselves.

20:20 FORESIGHT

What part can technology play in bridging the gap between consumer and the switch solution?

KEEP IT SIMPLE

HAVE AN INNOVATION PIPELINE

Companies get so focussed on the initial switch that they don't recognise that this is only the first step in the journey. They tend to leave any thought about the product pipeline until the first switch has happened. I can understand why this occurs but the earlier the new product pipeline is established then the quicker the line extension to market. In particular, planning to get a product to GSL should be included in the switch product design in the first place.

"with more than one player in a category, the market will develop a lot quicker than with just one brand on a mission."

COMPETITION

Controversially, I think that the market absolutely needs competition and choice to drive awareness and uptake. I have a theory that with more than one player in a category, the market will develop a lot quicker than with just one brand on a mission. Look at the evolution of Formula 1 (F1) and the technology for cycling in the Olympic Games

20:20 HINDSIGHT

Wyeth pulled the switch of their proton pump inhibitor (PPI) Zoton, leaving Zanprol to trail blaze the PPI category on its own. What if they had carried on their launch giving the pharmacist the option of two PPIs in their armoury. Would this have made a difference?

It is really hard being a brand owner in a one-horse race so maybe exclusivity in the market is less important in switching - consumers in the 21st century like choice.

Position right and execute brilliantly - bring it on.

HURDLES

Each country has its own unique healthcare system and reimbursement criteria for healthcare services - both factors that are likely to impact the uptake of switch products. There are a number of hurdles to overcome when switching medicines in the UK that should be taken account of in the thinking when planning a switch. Here are a few examples:-

There may be an obvious need for your switch in terms of prevalence of a condition or a high incidence of people at risk, but remember that people interested in buying a switch product are likely to be the people who to want to look after their health and are prepared to pay a contribution towards maintaining it. In some cases they may be those likely to be least at risk.

90% of prescriptions in England are issued free of charge, while in Scotland and Wales prescriptions are free. In England, there is a standard fee charged for prescriptions per item dispensed[21] which sets the mindset, especially for pharmacists, for how much an over-the-counter medicine should cost for those who have to pay, even though the prescription charge itself bears absolutely no relation to the cost of the drug.

In the UK only 5-10% of the revenue of an independent pharmacy is derived from over-the-counter medicines sales. Instead, the business priority for them is the dispensing business.

Pharmacists tend to start their recommendations with the least effective product and then trading them up through levels rather than going for the highest efficacy as first line.[34]

"In the UK only 5-10% of the revenue of an independent pharmacy is derived from over-the-counter medicines sales."

With more complex switches, pharmacists are beginning to question their legal liability position and refer to the doctor in the first instance rather than take the risk of recommending inappropriately.

Pharmacists need to be engaged as partners in some way to avoid their natural default setting as gate-keeper and referrer.

Rather than embracing switch, doctors in general practice have not supported the most recent ones, putting out negative messages at the emergence of the product. This merely serves to fuel concerns, disengage pharmacists and put off potential early adopters.

It is really hard to persuade someone to purchase a drug that they need to take every day for a condition that is asymptomatic.

THINK ABOUT THE GAME CHANGERS

What if the prescription charge in England was abolished and replaced with a flat fee for visiting the doctor, as is the case in Ireland?

What if only generic medicines and those still with a patent were reimbursed by the NHS and branded prescription medicines could be advertised to the public, allowing them to buy them at a premium over the RX charge if they desired, as happens in the US?

What if doctor's receptionists encouraged callers to first visit their pharmacist for a consultation before making an appointment?

What if all medicines were made available for consumers to self- select in the pharmacy? (This will be a possibility for some pharmacies from October 2013 in the UK and is the current modus operandi in the US.)

What if some conditions became self care zones that doctors proactively promoted to their patients?

"Why not consider the possibility of piloting the Switch in the UK? If you can make a Switch work in the UK then there may be a platform to build a case for Switch in other countries. In any case it is an opportunity to build some sales and generate some metrics in a real-life setting in a territory and get the proof of principle ironed out."

Anna Maxwell

Chapter 5

SWITCH POTENTIAL

This chapter considers the different options available for switching medicines and is designed to stimulate thinking around switch.

Given the challenges of running switch projects in Europe and the cost of launching a switch in the US, this chapter also explores the possibility of piloting switch projects in the UK where the regulator is switch friendly and the consumer is sophisticated and distribution channels well defined.

7 SWITCH OPTIONS

There at at least seven different options for switch illustrated in this chapter.

1. Status change.

2. Me Too.

3. New Molecule.

4. New Supply Model.

5. New Indication.

6. New strength or format.

7. Switching a molecule you don't own.

THE SWITCH POTENTIAL

We are now working in an era where it is said that most of the easy switches have been done - but there are still possibilities for simple switches when companies mine for them. There are around 2000 prescription-only molecules in the UK compared to 500 pharmacy-only molecules and 900 GSL molecules[16].

DIFFERENT TYPES OF SWITCH

Thinking laterally, there are many options for evolving switch projects and some of the options are outlined in the table below. I use this type of framework when mining a portfolio for switch candidates: -

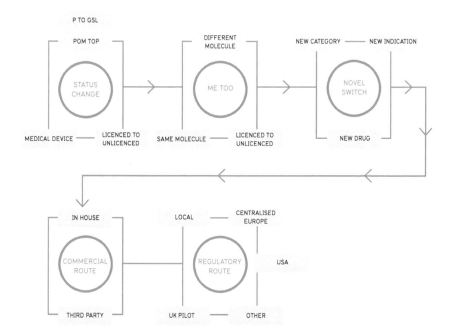

Here is an explanation of the table left: -

1. STATUS CHANGE

In the UK there are a number of routes possible for changing the status of a medicine. The route chosen depends upon the start point of the molecule, ie the current legal status of the product (see Table Page 18).

a. POM to P Switch – this is where a molecule with a prescription-only status is converted into a pharmacy-only status which can then be supplied by the pharmacist. This type of switch involves the submission of a relevant application to the regulatory body. Sometime it is the indication that has to be switched, eg thrush (see point 5 on page 74.)

b. P to GSL Switch – when a product moves from a pharmacy-supervised status to a General Sales List (GSL) status that enables self-selection and the opening up of new distribution channels such as supermarkets. This type of switch involves the submission of a relevant application to the regulatory body.

Note: In the US, switches are made from Rx to OTC. There is presently no P category and therefore products switch from prescription-only straight to self-selection over the counter (OTC). This type of switch involves the submission of a relevant application to the US Food and Drug Administration (FDA).

c. Licensed to medical device status – In Europe, the regulation of Medical Devices[17] is different to medicines in that a CE mark is required, which is obtained from a competent authority. There are specific controls around manufacture, supply and labelling that must be followed.

One benefit of a medical device route is that the labelling has to include a medical claim. This has the potential of making the medical device a stronger proposition than it would be if a food or cosmetic and almost equivalent to a Marketing Authorisation status. An example of this type of switch is GSL to medical device, eg skin barrier creams.

Note: Medical devices have no pharmacologic effect, metabolic or immunological effect. They prevent or treat conditions through physical, mechanical, thermal, physico-chemical or chemical action, for example barrier creams, weight management products.

d. A medicine status to unlicensed cosmetic[18] or food[19] product – Moving a product from licensed to unlicensed status saves the costs of managing and keeping updated the marketing authorisation which companies are obliged to do with a licensed product; however, the strength of the claims are diluted and marketing becomes more challenging. This type of switch is simple to undertake without reference to the medicines authority. Examples of this type of switch are GSL to food supplement, eg certain vitamins, GSL to cosmetic, eg mouthwashes.

2. ME TOO

Where the molecule has already been switched and the new product is a copy of an existing switched product, eg cetirizine for a private label or omeprazole as a brand extension.

3. NEW MOLECULE

Where the indication has already switched and the new molecule is a better clinical option or has a better efficacy or safety profile or just a different molecule to that was the first to switch in the category, eg fexofenadine/hayfever.

4. NEW SUPPLY MODEL

Where the molecule has already been switched but a new supply model is developed that is an enhanced version of the first generation model, perhaps simplifying the process for the sale, the label, or enables the pharmacist consultation to be done in a different way, eg a revised pharmacy protocol for tamsulosin or sumatriptan.

5. NEW CATEGORY OR NEW INDICATION

Where the switch of the molecule opens up a new opportunity for self-medication or prevention of disease, such as prevention of osteoporosis or over-active bladder. Companies may also be able to employ the use of the molecule in a different way such as exploiting a known side effect, eg sleep, or promoting an off-label use, eg hair re-growth, thus inventing new self-medication possibilities.

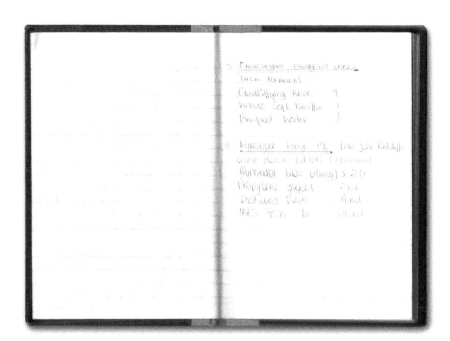

Early recipe for minoxidol lotion 1% (Regaine) to treat male pattern baldness as an off label indication, minoxidil is a cardiovascular drug for hypertension. I frequently made this up in the pharmacy in Oxford where I worked during my early career as a pharmacist.

6. NEW STRENGTH OR FORMAT

Where the proposed switch is a different strength or delivery format to the current switch version, eg Orlistat 120mg (Rx) and Alli 60mg (OTC)

7. COMMERCIAL ROUTE

The commercial route adopted may also give further options:

(i) In-house Switch – Switching a molecule that the company already owns.

(ii) Third-party Licence – Switching a molecule that is owned by someone else and licensed in for the purpose.

Option ii. may have significant benefits in that the third-party molecule may be competitively advantaged compared to the in-house option, eg higher up the treatment algorithm, better safety profile, bigger potential, different category.

One example of a third-party licence is when The Royal Pharmaceutical Society of Great Britain rather than the brand owner Bayer brought about the clotrimazole switch. More details on this case study can be found at www.dynamicswitch. co.uk.

THE UK AS A TEST MARKET?

Why not consider the possibility of piloting the switch in the UK? If you can make a switch work in the UK then there may be a platform to build a case for switch in other countries. In any case it is an opportunity to build some sales and generate some metrics in a real-life setting in a territory and get the proof of principle ironed out. Evidence of use on the OTC setting from other markets is very useful in determining the risks and benefits of switching medicines and now regulatory agencies worldwide want to see this information if it exists.

The UK's National Health Service offers free healthcare provision, thus making it probably one of the hardest markets in which to persuade people to self-medicate. When it was set up in the late 1940s, the NHS was designed to be free at the point of need, yet it has become free at the point of delivery, ie to everyone who accesses it. So it doesn't have a value to most who use it until they develop a serious life-threatening condition, need an operation or lose their mobility and independence. With an ageing population and increased life expectancy of the nation going forward, the numbers don't stack up and something has to change. I believe that switch should be part of the NHS re-engineering process.

In light of this economical situation with the NHS, the UK regulatory authority MHRA is very receptive to widening access to medicines and increasing the choice for patients; because of this, the UK is viewed as a world leading country in switch. MHRA are receptive to conversations about the possibilities for switch and this can easily be arranged in the early stages of switch evaluation before any significant investment is committed.

MHRA also has a clearly defined process for switch (which is used by other countries as a basis for their switch framework) available at www.mhra.gov.uk.

The benefits of running a switch pilot in the UK are:

- It has a sizeable population, the third-largest self care business in Europe. [20]
- There are large and small pharmacy chains and networks that can be partners in the delivery of the switch programme.
- There is advanced technology to capture sales data.
- Internet pharmacy is well established for mail-order supply.
- The legislative environment is receptive to switch.
- There is reduced complexity associated with a UK switch compared to a centralised European one.
- It is quicker.

20:20 HINDSIGHT

How different could it have been for Pfizer if a UK pilot had been possible for sildenafil (Viagra) instead of a centralised European procedure?

"Don't hesitate to hire in independent switch expertise to help design and set up your switch project from the start. There needs to be some experience of running switch projects on the core team. People who know about switch can influence the timeline, coach around road blocks, provide insight and help decision-making, while at the same time maintaining the project's momentum."

Anna Maxwell

SWITCH DYNAMICS

Chapter 6
GREAT EXPECTATIONS

PLANNING A SWITCH

Welcome to the practical part of Switch Dynamics. If you are just starting at this point then the previous chapters cover information, theory and case studies around switch, which you may find helpful. The rest of the book deals with the practical aspects of switch, looks at what you need to do to get started, defines roles and responsibilities of the various players and suggests a way to effectively and efficiently run switch projects in large and small organisations.

Before you start on this section, I recommend that you read each of the chapter summaries in Chapters 1, 2 and 3 and also Chapter 4 in full as this gives an overview of the types of switches that are possible. Having done this, you will more easily be able to identify what type of switch you may be dealing with. This will give you a valuable baseline of information about switching medicines before you embark on your journey.

Summary

A switch comprises a number of projects undertaken in series and parallel.
The work-streams involved are interrelated and interdependent.
It is a dynamic process; it is not chronological.
You need:.

A master plan.

A core team and a project leader.

Advice from people who know about switching medicines.

A navigator.

Multi-disciplinary input from medical, regulatory, healthcare, professionals, pharmacists and marketing at the start.

A ring-fenced budget.

A long-term view.

HAVE YOU GOT A SWITCHER?

In the previous sections we have covered the background to switch, why it is important in the healthcare equation and how it can be used as an innovation stream to deliver incremental sales and growth. We also looked at the different types of switch and the possible avenues for mining opportunities. Now we want to consider how to unlock the potential of a switcher.

The key to successful switch is to explore the possibilities, understand the journey and develop a master plan. This involves having the right team and stakeholders on board, asking the right questions at the right time, getting the design of the switch product right at the outset and understanding the obstacles and hurdles along the way.

If you don't have switch experience in your team, then you will need to hire in switch specific expertise; by this I mean people who have done switches before and can, with the benefit of experience, help design and activate the product in line with your company objectives. They can also objectively help, plan, track and navigate the switch project to help it fit within your company process.

"Switch is a stepped process, with distinct phases that are interrelated and interdependent. Each phase is easy to implement once you have a core team and they have put together the master plan."

Switcher – branded or generic drug molecule combined with an idea for a self care application.

SWITCH START UP

Switch is a stepped process, with distinct phases that are interrelated and interdependent. Each phase is easy to implement once you have a core team and they have put together the master plan.

As with any new product development project, there are various work-streams involved and these need to be initiated as part of the plan at the relevant stage. Key to minimising the time it takes to switch the molecule is to initiate some of these pieces of work in series and some in parallel. It is not a chronological process.

7 PHASES OF A PERFECT SWITCH

MISSION CRITICAL

You need to identify the team involved at each stage in advance, let them know who they are, what is expected from them and force the timeline for the project into their schedules. This automatically creates the process to get things done. This has to be their Mission Critical.

It is vital to get local marketing, regulatory, medical, key opinion leader and pharmacist input up front in the first few weeks of the project for the concept-shaping stages. This allows the best positioning and regulatory rationale to be developed, thus harnessing the insight that already exists on the ground.

The best way of doing this is to undertake a collaborative marketing and regulatory and medical affairs discussion with input from key opinion leaders, pharmacists and people who know about switch.

Strong leadership, decision-making and an ability to delegate are required. The core team need to be empowered, with the ability to be flexible and think laterally: you will be surprised that even for the best-planned switch projects there will be things that come in from left of field when the submission hits the regulator, at the public consultation or in the market place. Such obstacles have to be navigated quickly and efficiently to keep the project on track.

CHICKEN OR EGG?

OK. So you want to switch a product but where do you start? There may be various situations that you find yourself in: -

- We have a molecule coming off patent soon within our Rx portfolio and we would like to see if this has potential for switch.
- We have a large portfolio of molecules: is there anything that could be switched?
- We operate in a number of categories and we would like to consider switching possibilities for those.
- We would like to create a new self care category for this condition. What are the possibilities for switch?
- My corporate colleagues want to explore the possibilities to switch this drug in our market.
- We have begun to put together our proposal for a switch but we have hit a roadblock.

THE CORE TEAM

The first step is to identify a core team and buy the project time by forcing a timeline through the organisation. This will give the switch project momentum. In the early stage, unless you set about creating a dedicated switch team (the optimum scenario), then it is most likely that the core team will be a virtual team. A focussed two hours with three, well-briefed and up-to-speed people on a virtual team is almost a full-time equivalent day. There is a lot that you can get done with leadership and a virtual team who focus on getting things done in a few dedicated hours per week.

DEFINE THE TEAM

If the project is corporate run, the core team should at least engage local marketing, medical and regulatory experts from each relevant market from the start. What I mean by this is that people on the ground in the country/countries where the switch will take place should be involved in the project from Day 1.

This is often the first mistake that is made in switch projects and it creates the possibility for key decisions to be made at a global level that may not be workable in practice. Usually these are not discovered until much later in the process, by which time they are really difficult to unravel - and this ultimately holds up the project.

Local country teams should also be supported by their own key opinion leaders who represent the real-life situation in their market. The core team also need support from people who have done switches before and who know about the intricacies of the switch process in their specific market. This could be internal support from a project sponsor or an injection of expertise from a switch navigation expert.

SWITCH CORE TEAM STRUCTURE

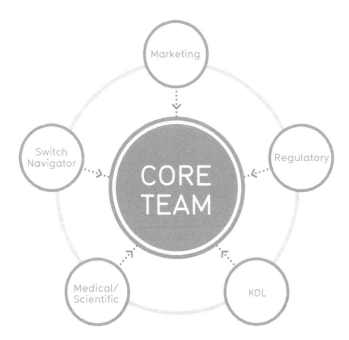

If you plan to run a global project then one suggested structure is to have a corporate team which is mirrored with sub-teams from each territory. these teams can all be connected by virtual communication streams set up so that each discipline can keep apprised of what is happening in each territory, allowing them to support each other, cross-fertilise ideas and solve problems

GLOBAL SWITCH PROJECT STRUCTURE EXAMPLE

Today's technology makes this communication and model entirely possible. It doesn't have to take up lots of time, either; it is the way that the communication sessions are set up and run that is key. Making each team member summarise in a three-minute update and rigidly stick to it is a good discipline to follow.

WHAT SKILLS AND EXPERIENCE SHOULD BE ON THE CORE TEAM?

You need to make your best talent available, with a mix of skills and disciplines led by a project leader. There also need to be visionaries and innovators within the switch resource pool - people who have the ability to think outside the box and solve problems. The core team has to have a command of the regulatory process, the switch journey, what is involved and when. They also have to be capable of figuring out the consumer pathway and remain sensitive to the needs of the different stakeholders such as pharmacists and doctors.

"Like a mother ship with pods – the sub teams replicate the Global Team in terms of members (see diagram left) – held together by communication and able to transfer ideas"

They have to be decisive, determined and resilient and believe in the project. There is no place for negativity on the core team; however, detractors do have a place on the periphery because if you can overcome their objections there will be a better outcome for the project. Use their objections as a market research tool - it is the best advice you will get.

WHAT IS THE ROLE OF THE CORE TEAM?

The core team sets the direction for the switch project in their territory. They have day-to-day accountability for the general running of it, the decisions taken, momentum and the achievement of the milestones.

It is the core team's responsibility to work up the detail of the switch master plan. Together they consider options and define and deploy resources, engaging the assets necessary at the appropriate time. They monitor and demonstrate progress, manage expectations and take corrective actions where and when necessary. They communicate their progress regularly in an agreed way within the organisation.

We will talk about stakeholders and their management in a later chapter. However, it is the core team's responsibility to build and sustain rapport with stakeholders, which is best achieved on a peer-to-peer basis. If you are talking to medics, for example, then it is a good idea to be able to talk medic to medic on the same level.

Summary of core team accountabilities

- Set direction.
- Have day-to-day accountability.
- Deploy assets.
- Overcome hurdles.
- Build and sustain rapport with stakeholders.
- Demonstrate progress.
- Monitor and correct.
- Manage expectations.

APPOINT A LEADER

Sometimes it falls to the marketing team member to lead and motivate the core team but this doesn't always have to be the case. The project leader for a switch project must be given the time in their day job to devote to it and that means allocating a small amount of time every day.

These individuals should be organised, good at planning, capable of managing multilevel projects they need to infuse enthusiasm and motivate and bringing people along on the ride. They must be able to facilitate and guide discussions to a conclusion, good at stepping back, good at delegating. The project leader is responsible for pulling together the master plan, hitting the milestones and facilitating the communication channels.

Useful skills for a switch project leader

- Experienced Project Manager.
- Pioneer.
- Thinks outside the box.
- Keeps a clear head.
- Organised.
- Balanced.
- Makes decisions.
- Gets things done.
- Motivates others.

OK, so I have these people on my team but what are they supposed to be doing?

The core project team is responsible for all decisions in their territory and facilitating the work to make the switch happen on time and to maintain a momentum. The one thing I have learned is that time can easily slip away and you cannot get it back. Delaying on the appointment of an asset because they are waiting to start on receipt of a purchase order can set you back six weeks, which just puts the commercial realisation of the project further and further into the future. It's easy to lose six months this way. That's why the Core Project Team have to make this their Mission Critical and act on road-blocks, administration, obstacles and hurdles with urgency.

Lets have a look at the specific responsibilities of each member of the core team:-

REGULATORY

Put simply, regulatory are the guardians of the rationale for the switch. They are tasked with establishing the workable criteria for the switch, in collaboration with the rest of the core team, ie, medical, marketing and other relevant stakeholders. Decisions made at this stage could impact the label, the Rx product or the advertising communication so it is important to spend time working through the implications and looking at the switch from a 360° perspective and working out what it is going to look like in practice.

They are also responsible for defining the regulatory strategy and navigating the regulatory process. The regulatory lead is responsible for preparing the submission for the switch that goes to the authorities and liaising with them through the process.

MEDICAL/SCIENTIFIC

Medical and scientific expertise is the cornerstone of the switch strategy, crucial to creating differentiating claims and the label for the switch. These people come up with the medical and scientific rationale that underpins the switch and the scientific evidence for the basis of it.

They also build relationships with Key Opinion Leaders and maintain them through the process. Usually they are able to mine nuggets of insight from current clinical practice, which is where cross-fertilisation of ideas is powerful. Between territories, for example, the way a molecule is used in another market with different regulatory restrictions can open up opportunities.

Sometimes these can be throw-away comments, eg "In the US physicians use our sample pack as an immediate dose that the patient takes because the first line drug takes a couple of days to work." This knowledge could provide a great short-term treatment for an acute condition, making it perfect for self care.

MARKETING

This is the team that brings the idea to life: it is up to marketing to find a workable positioning that is compelling enough so that a person wants to buy the product and feels confident enough to use it in the self care setting and continue to do so.

They are also responsible for the naming, branding and visual identity, assessing feasibility and commercial viability, gathering the appropriate insight, co-ordinating the relevant training, the go to market plan, communications strategy, any advertising and promotion and related products and services. Marketing facilitate the implementation and activation of the products when the time arrives, track against the success criteria and determine the innovation stream.

KEY OPINION LEADERS

These people are crucial to the success of the project. Ideally, you need a specialist consultant, a GP and a pharmacist available to bounce ideas off in the early stage. Usually they are individuals who are accomplished in their field and would be drawn from a pool of medical doctors and consultants with a specialism in the therapeutic category in which you are switching. The consultant is important because support is necessary for the regulatory submission and the clinical expert statements that accompany it.

Sometimes there is also a charity or self-help group that can be involved. These people can help shape the strategy in the early stages, overcoming any obstacles and providing the evidence and rationale to support the switch. They need to be retained in the early stages of the project, to be on the end of the phone and to provide support all the way through the process.

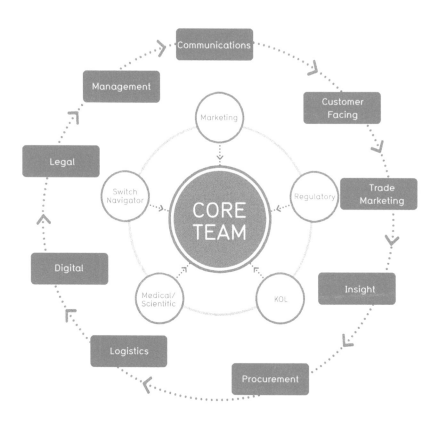

THE WIDER TEAM

The internal wider team

There is a wider team that will need to be engaged during the later stages of
the project but it is wise to think about who those might be and plan when they
need to be engaged. In larger organisations these would typically include
Procurement, Communications, Logistics, Commercial, Consumer Insight and
Sales Colleagues. It is worth preparing them well in advance.

Project sponsor

Invariably there will be a project sponsor who oversees the project and takes an
interest. Usually this is a senior manager or director who is not involved in the
day-to-day running of the business but may have some sort of accountability for
it later on in the process. These people are busy and their time is golden so use
them wisely to help make the right key decisions or when you hit a roadblock.

Switch expertise

Don't hesitate to hire in independent switch expertise to help design and set up your switch project from the start. There needs to be some experience of running switch projects on the core team. People who know about switch can influence the timeline, coach around road blocks, provide insight and help decision-making, while at the same time maintaining the project's momentum.

The external wider team

No matter how small your organisation, it is inevitable that you are going to need to hire some specialist agencies and services to help you in this project from concept to launch. If you have a procurement process then you need to build time for the procurement team to do their due diligence around suitable suppliers. I recommend planning three months ahead for this.

Likely service organisations required, preferably with experience of switching medicines

"It is like preparing a team for the Olympics…"

Anna Maxwell

Chapter 7

RUNNING A SWITCH PROJECT

This chapter is a quick start guide for running a switch project if you are chosen as a project leader. It covers getting started with your core team, includes what should typically feature in a switch master plan and outlines the work streams involved.

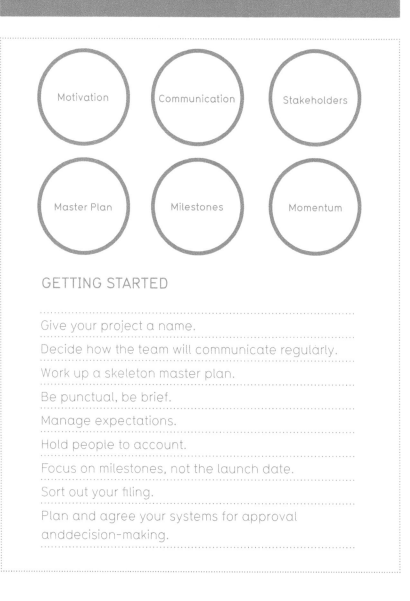

Motivation

Communication

Stakeholders

Master Plan

Milestones

Momentum

GETTING STARTED

Give your project a name.

Decide how the team will communicate regularly.

Work up a skeleton master plan.

Be punctual, be brief.

Manage expectations.

Hold people to account.

Focus on milestones, not the launch date.

Sort out your filing.

Plan and agree your systems for approval anddecision-making.

THE PROJECT LEADER

Running a switch project is like preparing a team for the Olympics. It is up to the project leader to lead and motivate the core team and, importantly, make sure that you are hitting milestones.

It is also the project leader's responsibility to bring in the resources to support the team when they are required, identify any gaps in skills or expertise and plug them. Set up and directed properly, the project will shortly begin to maintain a perpetual momentum that is highly rewarding for those involved.

Another critical element of the project leader's role is to communicate the successes and challenges for the project on a formal regular basis. For best results it is a good idea to agree with peers and colleagues the procedure for internal communication up and down the line early on.

"It is a complicated process and there is a negotiation with the authorities that must take place. Success at the regulatory stage is not guaranteed"

MAKE YOUR PROJECT MISSION CRITICAL

Getting started.
- Identify who is on the core team.
- Get them together.
- Tell them about the process.
- Engage them in defining their roles.
- Agree their accountabilities.
- Allocate time in their diaries.
- Decide how and when they are going to communicate.

There are some simple tips to help achieve momentum from the start.

1. Give your project a name so people in your company can talk about it in confidence without having to explain every time – a good first task for the core team.

2. Prepare a skeleton project plan and work out the key milestones for each stage by working with and gathering relevant input from core team members.

3. Force a regular weekly telecon through the diary for the core team – this only has to be 45 minutes long.

4. Create a core agenda for this telecon, eg Actions Arising, Regulatory Update, Stakeholders, Project Plan and send by noon the day before.

5. Start the meeting on time – be there early. Ask for any additional points for the Agenda at the start of the meeting.

6. Appoint a team member (or you) to make brief bullet point actions with accountabilities and deadline and circulate them to the core team immediately after the telecon.

7. Keep to time - crack through the agenda on the day and be prepared to advise core team members to liaise outside the meeting if discussions on a particular topic run on.

8. Make decisions and demonstrate progress.

9. Nail people in terms of their action points, what are they going to do and by when.

10. Liaise with core team members during the week to keep them motivated and focused.

11. Celebrate success.

SWITCH FIT

12. **Reflect - Are the Core Team Switch Fit?**
     - Are they up for it?
     - Do they have the right skills, competencies and expertise?
     - Have they got the time?
     - What do they need?

THE SWITCH MASTER PLAN

Every switch project is unique and will typically include the following elements: -

MAJOR WORK STREAMS FROM START UP TO IMPLEMENTATION

MANAGING INTERNAL EXPECTATIONS

Just because there is a switch project in progress and a company has decided to devote resource to it, does not mean to say that the switch will happen any time soon. It is a complicated process and there is a negotiation with the authorities that must take place. Success at the regulatory stage is not guaranteed and there is a lot of work to be getting on with in the meantime and in preparation for optimising the time to market once the MA is granted.

One of the keys to running a successful project is being able to maintain positive momentum and hit the milestones but if you keep these to yourself then no one will know about the progress you are making. So it is important to communicate regularly.

"There is always too much enthusiasm to talk about launch date up front and the milestone fast becomes a millstone,"

Communication needs to be kept upbeat, with well-constructed messages to demonstrate your command of the situation. An agreed process for communication is best hammered out up front with the core team and internal stakeholders. This avoids the rumour mill starting up, especially when roadblocks occur at which point detractors are usually too ready to jump in with their contribution to add more spin.

There is always too much enthusiasm to talk about launch date up front and the milestone fast becomes a millstone, especially when commercial expectations are overlaid. It is almost as if once a company has decided to switch a molecule they fall into " it's a done deal mode" without considering that they are at the beginning of the process and there are no guarantees.

Whilst the project is in the regulatory process this is completely outside the control of the company and although there are undertakings for timelines given by the authorities, you should be aware that when they come back to you for more information their clock stops. It only restarts again when you respond to their request and each time there is a further request it can mean a three-month delay. So in my view, always heavily caveat any discussions around launch windows and focus everyone on the next milestone and broad target launch windows, eg first half or second half of the year.

TOP TIPS FOR RUNNING THE BEST SWITCH UPDATES

To get the best out of meetings and drive efficiency they should be Agenda driven.

Run through the project plan, focusing on the progress and stage you are at, review the timeline, identify any gaps or obstacles and highlight any resource requirements needed.

Agree up front the key messages on project status to be disseminated to the rest of the organisation.

Following the meeting prepare a short 1 or 2 slide presentation. Make it easy for your boss to pass on the messages - keep it simple.

SYSTEMS

Keeping track of any project requires attention to detail and it is a good idea for the project leader to think about how the company record of this project will be kept and where. Give some thought to filing key documents and set up the files and appropriate access within your organisation. There may be a protocol within your company so make sure that you are aware of it.

We work in a highly regulated environment and it surprises me that any pharmaceutical company still use job bag systems for the approval of their packaging and copy approval systems when there are electronic systems in existence around that make the process simple, efficient and more robust.

I have worked with Zinc Maps[22] which is bespoke to the life science industry and it turned copy approval from a time-consuming chore into a look forward to experience. It saves time by the bucket load and genuinely improves the quality of the work because you want to spend more time on it.

Documents are uploaded as PDFs (we got our agencies to do this at the start of the process) and then can be circulated to the relevant approvers who are licensed to use the system. The approver can actually make comments and mark up the document, working on the version with the latest comments. What's great about it is that you can see the comments that every one has made, there is an audit trail, and the final versions of the documents are archived for future reference.

Another benefit of an electronic system forces you to set up a process with accountabilities. Some companies have 2 rounds within their process, others 3, each with different levels of approvers coming into the process at various stages. Use a RACI (see below) or similar model.

You should also establish for your project some rules about approvals so that those involved with the process devote quality time to the first round and dump their comments on the first draft. Comments on the second draft should be by exception and reserved for grammatical errors, typos and anything that would cause a regulatory problem. If approvers are giving the process quality time on round one, the bulk of comment should be picked up on round 1, thus saving time later on.

RACI [25]

Responsible
Those who do the work to achieve the task.

Accountable (also *approver* or final *approving authority*.) The one ultimately answerable for the correct and thorough completion of the deliverable or task, and the one from whom *responsible* is delegated the work An accountable must sign off (approve) on work that *responsible* provides. There **must** be only one *accountable* specified for each task or deliverable.

Consulted (sometimes *counsel*)
Those whose opinions are sought, typically subject matter experts; and with whom there is two-way communication.

Informed
Those who are kept up-to-date on progress, often only on completion of the task or deliverable; and with whom there is just one-way communication.

OTHER SYSTEMS

There are quite a few project management software applications around which can help the project planning process and help keep you on track. Rather than creating one big Project Implementation Plan (PIP) with thousands of lines on it, I recommend breaking the project down into a series of smaller projects, each with timelines and milestones – Work stream Implementation Plan (WIP). There are good reasons for this:

It is easier to demonstrate progress and build a sense of achievement with a series of linked smaller plans.

It is more motivating to work on something that seems achievable and time bound.

You are more likely to make it happen with a set of smaller plans in bite-sized plans.

PITFALLS

AVOID THESE PITFALLS

- Heads not in the game.
- Poor communication.
- Thinking chronological timelines.
- Committing to a launch date too early.
- Forgetting about stakeholders.
- Not getting the positioning right .
- Not talking to pharmacists.
- Losing people from the core team.

"It is a good idea to come up with a few options for the supply model and not just the obvious one that is a hybrid of the GP scenario."

Anna Maxwell

Chapter 8

DESIGNING THE PROTOTYPE

This chapter looks at some of the different models that have been used in the pharmacy setting in the UK for switching medicines. It gives advice on how to design a prototype and the factors that are usually included in the commercial assessment in the early stages.

Summary

1. The best way of designing a prototype is to get out there and talk to a few GPs, KOLs, pharmacists and expert patients about it.

2. It is a good idea to come up with a few options for the supply model, not just the obvious one that is a hybrid of the GP scenario.

3. The newly adopted *"VALUE TREE FRAMEWORK"*[65] benefit:risk assessment tool can be used as an initial screening aid in assessing feasibility of a switch and throughout the switch process to sense check options.

4. From a commercial perspective significant unmet need is a useful criteria but there are others such as a better efficacy compared to existing alternatives.

5. The switch protocol has to be capable of becoming intuitive for the pharmacist, given the right training.

6. Any switch must be simple for the consumer to understand.

7. There are a number of different switch models
    a. Indication-led
    b. Risk factor-led
    c. Preventive
    d. Medical diagnosis
    e. Test and Treat
    f. Questionnaire-led
    g. Shared care
    h. Self-selection

8. Conventional market research may be misleading. In groundbreaking switches you have to work out what is going to happen in real life – how do people and stakeholders behave?

9. Set up the Intellectual Property early on: Name, Visual Identity, Website, URLs, etc.

10. Work out the deal breakers for the project up front.

DESIGNING THE PROTOTYPE

When it comes to ways to approach switch projects, you can either address a con-dition that would be suitable for self care, which could be an existing category or a new one. Or you could start with a molecule or portfolio of molecules that you want to screen. (see Chapter 5)

Quite a few companies begin with the latter situation, where they screen a wide portfolio of molecules. The disadvantage of this is that it takes for ever to plough through the list and decisions are slow. My advice is to work on groups of 3 to 5 molecules at a time, work out the criteria that would make them candidates up front, assess them and then move them on to the next stage. If you wait to finish the list before coming up with conclusions, it will take a long time and every day that passes is a day further to market.

"Ideally, the method of supply needs to be kept as simple as possible; if all this can be dealt with on the label then that is the optimal scenario."

HOW TO SCREEN A MOLECULE?

There is much theory about this and various methods including a recently pub-lished "Value Tree Framework" [24] that has been adopted by the UK regulator in their guidelines which considers the benefits and risks for non-prescription med-icines (see diagram). It is designed from a regulatory, decision-making perspec-tive rather than a commercial one.

The benefit:risk assessment tool can be used as an initial screening aid in assess-ing feasibility of a switch and throughout the switch process to sense check op-tions. One benefit is that it will identify incremental benefits and risks as different factors are modified. Another benefit is that it can also act to facilitate a discus-sion with the competent authority, eg MHRA.

Value tree framework of benefits and risks for non-prescription medicines. –
Triptan Example

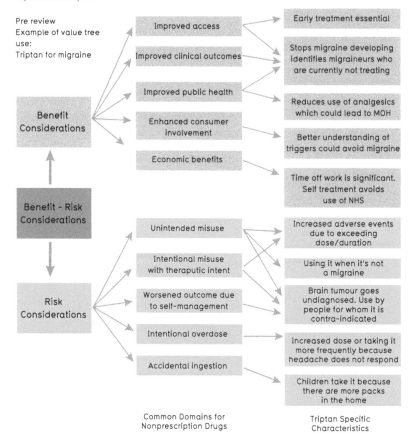

Pre review
Example of value tree
use:
Triptan for migraine

Benefit Considerations

Benefit - Risk Considerations

Risk Considerations

Improved access → Early treatment essential

Improved clinical outcomes → Stops migraine developing, identifies migraineurs who are currently not treating

Improved public health

Enhanced consumer involvement → Reduces use of analgesics which could lead to MOH

Better understanding of triggers could avoid migraine

Economic benefits → Time off work is significant. Self treatment avoids use of NHS

Unintended misuse → Increased adverse events due to exceeding dose/duration

Intentional misuse with theraputic intent → Using it when it's not a migraine

Worsened outcome due to self-management → Brain tumour goes undiagnosed. Use by people for whom it is contra-indicated

Intentional overdose → Increased dose or taking it more frequently because headache does not respond

Accidental ingestion → Children take it because there are more packs in the home

Common Domains for Nonprescription Drugs

Triptan Specific Characteristics

Brass, E.P., R. Lofstedt, and O. Renn, Improving the Decision-Making Process for Nonprescription
Drugs: A Framework for Benefit-Risk Assessment. Clin Pharmacol Ther, 2011. 90(6): p. 791-803.

Triptan example reproduced with kind permission of PAGB www.pagb.co.uk
Look up more examples at www.dynamicswitch.co.uk

Although useful, the Value Tree Framework is only one tool and companies need
to use a mix of tools, their own decision-making processes, research, stakeholder
input and other activities to assess the feasibility of the switch and the investment
required to make the vision a reality.

The best way of screening a molecule is to get out there and talk to a few GPs,
KOLs, pharmacists and expert patients about it to get their views and opinions on

a particular molecule or category and talk to them about the possibilities for self care. Usually the biggest concern is around safety, whether a member of the public can assess their own set of symptoms and what they might miss. There are also usually concerns about the pharmacist's ability to supply suitably and a lot of the discussion can be around missing a more serious condition, as well as misuse.

There is varied opinion regarding the suitability of the pharmacist to manage more complex conditions so don't be surprised by this. However, this it is just an obstacle - thinking should change over time as pharmacy evolves its role in primary care and builds meaningful services and support to GPs.

"some consideration needs to be given to the format of drugs that are intended to be taken over a lifetime to make compliance easier as well as the price."

Quite a bit of focus should be given to these initial scoping discussions, in particular looking at different possibilities for a switch. It is a good idea to come up with a few options for the supply model and not just the obvious one that is a hybrid of the GP scenario. Talk to a KOL for long enough and they will find a way to open up the possibilities, remove the barriers and jump the hurdles for OTC supply if that is what they are tasked to do.

There are lots of possibilities: lower dose, different format, initial diagnosis by the doctor, different indication, one-off doses, test and treat and many more. I am really intrigued by off-label uses for Rx products; there is untapped potential there that could be harnessed to build new OTC possibilities that haven't even been thought of yet.

ONE SIZE DOES NOT FIT ALL

As I have mentioned earlier it is vital to get input from the various disciplines that will be involved in the switch in the first stages so that the switch can be developed into some thing that is workable in the markets concerned. If you have accountability for a number of countries then because consumers have different attitudes and the healthcare systems disparate, one size does not fit all.

In my experience where a "global" approach is taken, there is a dumbing-down of the strategy or the positioning and everything becomes a compromise. Sometimes the switch just doesn't get off the drawing board. What tends to happen is that the regulatory team come up with a proposal based upon the existing prescription scenario in the largest market and that forces the design down a particular route that may not be the best workable solution for the commercial scenario. The regulatory submission gets written, a position adopted, rationale and switch criteria get set in tablets of stone that eventually end up impacting the label, the positioning or the advertising claim, all of which becomes sub-optimal.

Sometimes the marketing and commercial teams are only involved in the late stages, even after a submission has been made, and it is hard to come back from that position. Even worse is the case where marketing don't get the chance to look at the possibilities of what the switch could be.

Doing the work up front and talking to KOLs and stakeholders in local markets enable the compromises to be planned into the design into the regulatory strategy or the method of supply. It is better to get this sorted out in the beginning rather than to have to make U turns later. So it is a really good idea to get together and brainstorm the different options and possibilities that your switch could be right up front in the early stages and get engagement for the ideas across the functions and teams.

Ideally, the method of supply needs to be kept as simple as possible; if all this can be dealt with on the label then that is the optimal scenario. Significant unmet need is a useful driver but there are others such as a better drug compared to existing alternatives. The switch has to be capable of becoming intuitive for the pharmacist given the right training and simple for the consumer to understand.

There are various different models that are possible. Here are some examples:

There are various different models that are possible. Here are some examples

1. Indication-led – **where there are clear instructions about the symptoms, who it is for and under what circumstances**

2. Risk factor-led – **a group of people who have certain factors that predispose them to a condition, eg stroke**

3. Preventive – **for the prevention of the onset of a disease, eg osteoporosis**

4. Medical diagnosis – **where a consumer has already been diagnosed with a condition by a doctor, eg IBS**

5. Test and Treat – **where some kind of test to determine whether the patient needs the treatments is undertaken and the results assessed prior to the medicine being administered, eg Azithromycin for Chlamydia**

6. Questionnaire-led – **where the pharmacist runs through a checklist prior to supply to determine suitability for supply, eg sumatriptan**

7. Shared care – **where the pharmacist supplies on the basis of symptoms and the doctor diagnoses the condition, eg Tamsulosin**

8. Self-selection - **cimetidine**

Each of these methods has been tried in the UK with varying degrees of success:

1. Indication-led: The early switches such as Loperamide were against a clearly defined set of symptoms, eg acute diarrhoea, that is easily recognisable by the consumer. These are recognised as being the easiest switches because they are relatively simple self-limiting conditions with an easily recognisable set of symptoms that can be dealt with on the label. Loperamide itself was a superior next-generation treatment for diarrhoea, compared to kaolin and morphine.

- Loperamide Critical Success Factors. — **LOPERAMIDE**
- The inconvenience of the condition.
- Symptoms easily recognisable by the consumer.
- Emergency use – need it now.
- Self-limiting condition.
- Next generation: highly effective, fast-acting product.
- Medicine cabinet item "Just in case."
- Detailing force visiting pharmacy for peer-to-peer discussion.
- Rx heritage.
- Inferior Competition.

2. Risk factor-led: These switches are actually quite a hard sell because by assessing risk you are saying to a person that they might develop a more serious condition in the future so taking the drug becomes a kind of insurance policy to prevent this happening or slow the onset of the condition.

Usually in such cases there are not really any symptoms, although in the main there are issues relating to lifestyle that can be identified, eg high-sugar diet, BMI index, high cholesterol. In the case of statins, through finger prick testing of blood cholesterol levels, the impact of the statin can be measured and benefits demonstrated, as could metrics for people at risk of developing diabetes as part of an overall lifestyle programme. Maybe in the risk factor-led instances it is the programme or the test that carries the commercial value and the drug is not the main player, eg WeightWatchers + orlistat (Alli) combination.

I also think that some consideration needs to be given to the format of drugs that are intended to be taken over a lifetime to make compliance easier as well as the price. How widely would statins be used if they were prepared as a granular format to be sprinkled on food instead of table salt? – a Shake & Snack concept.[35]

4. Medical Diagnosis: Pharmacists are uncomfortable about this option because they have to take the patient's word for the fact that the doctor has already diagnosed the condition.

"Given the pressure on the healthcare system I cannot see why a pharmacist should not be enabled to sell medicines, for example for chronic conditions, once a person has been diagnosed."

With the introduction of electronic patient medication records and transparency of medicine history perhaps the anxieties around this will subside. Given the pressure on the healthcare system I cannot see why a pharmacist should not be enabled to sell medicines, for example for chronic conditions, once a person has been diagnosed. This could actually work out cheaper for the consumer than the prescription charge and in my view would start to change perceptions about self care and paying for certain medicines rather than getting them for free, eg inhalers. There would also be a cost saving in terms of surgery time and administration of the prescription-pricing process.

5. Test & Treat: Switches that have been set up to involve some kind of service seem to have worked better than questionnaire-led switches. This is really interesting because in the past, when pharmacists have been asked in research whether they want to be trained and accredited for certain medicines before they are able to supply them, the answer has been a resounding no. Yet, in reality the azithromycin (Clamelle) example proves the case that accreditation - far from alienating pharmacists - actually engages them. In the case of STI (Sexually Transmitted Infections) services, pharmacists have demonstrated that they are prepared to pay to be accredited.

The OTC Clamelle azithromycin model involves the purchase of a test by the consumer that is completed at home and sent to a lab for analysis. Results are then securely forwarded to a designated pharmacy where, upon receipt of a positive test result, the pharmacist can sell the drug treatment (an antibiotic) to the consumer and make an intervention for the partner if appropriate.

In order to become accredited to supply this service, the pharmacist has to register and pay to receive the training and offer the service. My assumption is that there are many more test kits sold than the drug itself and that both the sale of the test kit and sale of the drug deliver income for the pharmacy and to the brand owner.

What was different about this switch at launch was that the communication focused on raising awareness of the condition rather than the particular brand and focused on pushing the worried into pharmacy or to their GP to get tested for those who could not afford to purchase it. There also appeared to be early tie ups with local NHS initiatives generating a public health awareness campaign, giving credibility to the campaign and helping to push the message to a wider audience.

"it does demonstrate that where pharmacists have been engaged through their own investment in education and accreditation then they get behind a concept to make it work."

©NHS Greenwich Led Chlamydia Public Awareness Campaign www.checkurself.org.uk

This model is great news for switch. On the surface the protocol for supply is quite complex and would probably not research terribly well because it is ground breaking but it does demonstrate that where pharmacists have been engaged through their own investment in education and accreditation then they get behind a concept to make it work. There are other good examples of this in pharmacy, eg Lipotrim weight loss programme, which is not a switch but an accredited service that pharmacists elect and pay a fee to provide.

There are now two models for pharmacist remuneration for Chlamydia Services: the NHS-funded national chlamydia screening service for under 24 year olds where a Pharmacist receives a fee for performing the service and Actavis Clamelle test and treat service which is a private service for all ages. The pharmacist makes money on selling the test for about £25 and, if test results are positive, they also sell the tabs for around £25.

CRITICAL SUCCESS FACTORS FOR AZITHROMYCIN

- Pharmacy accreditation programme
- Pharmacy investment (time and money)
- Public Health awareness campaign initially a priority
- More commercial value in the test than treatment
- Low-key branding
- Actavis is a generics company which has a different profitability model compared to the typical OTC or Rx brand owner.

AZITHROMYCIN

SHARED CARE

A vision of a working partnership between GP and pharmacist with consumers who can recognise their symptoms and identify themselves. This is definitely something for the future when the technology enables consumers to self-triage and GPs let go of their stranglehold on certain groups of patients driven by the fact that the budget will not stretch to everybody.

It would be great if we could speed this process up now for the benefit of the public. Why should the pharmacist not be the first port of call for certain conditions? The shared-care model style for tamsulosin may be ahead of its time.

VISION FOR THE FUTURE

A future model for more complex switches could be one that uses technology to capture data from the consumer as a first step, with assessment and digital interventions as part of the interaction. Symptomatic or behavioural information could be obtained using digital or mobile technology and through electronic means a consumer dialogue becomes part of the process of engagement. At some point there could be an intervention via telehealth technology or even a digital doctor or other healthcare professional intervention.

In the case of prevention of disease, such technology could be used to capture personal information over time around risk factors so that an accurate picture of their behaviour can be gathered and a 360° assessment made by the healthcare professional. This enables a tailored programme to be put together that addresses their particular habits and behaviour pattern.

Such initiatives could be joined up to coaching and support being delivered via the web and also the online supply of the drug at regular intervals.

"technology enables consumers to self triage"

HOW TO DESIGN A PROTOTYPE FOR A SWITCH

1. Start with the Summary of Product Characteristics SmPC.

2. Consider in-use experience in other countries.

3. Look at clinical evidence and any off-label use that could potentially be supported.

4. Identify the direct and indirect competition and what they are doing or saying.

5. Look at possible OTC format options, eg dose, strength and pack size, as well as delivery system.

6. Are there any restrictions in use, eg age/duration?

7. Understand the current patient pathway in detail: what do they do?

8. Research around your topic to understand what really happens in practice.

9. Look for any support programmes or charity groups and find out what they do?

10. Work up at least three rough potential positioning ideas with claims and indications.

11. Work out how the consumer is going to access the medicine in the OTC setting – what is the process?

12. Work out why your plan won't work in practice – find solutions to address.

13. Talk to KOLs , GPs and pharmacists to get them to think of the possibilities.

14. Talk to the regulator using the Value Tree Framework [34] and get their input on claims and indications, the likely hurdles and objections, their thoughts on feasibility and how they would assess it. By doing this you will understand the process that they would adopt and their timelines.

15. Decide who it is for, why, how and when they should use it and sense-check by talking to a few consumers.

HOW TO ASSESS COMMERCIAL POTENTIAL OF PROTOTYPES

It is a good idea to agree the method by which you are going to evaluate the commercial potential of the switcher in advance - ie, before you get too deep into the process - and determine what the success criteria are for a molecule to proceed.

Every company has a different way of doing this and I don't believe that the conventional models applied to regular product launches, which aim accurately to forecast volume sales, can be applied to switch projects. That is because there are so many drivers in the unforeseen consequences category that it is extremely hard to predict what the outcome will be. Thus all forecasting models become an educated estimate based on the best assumptions but not on real test data.

At the ballpark level, a typical first-stage commercial assessment would include some or all of the criteria set out below. This type of analysis is useful for sifting priorities

TYPICAL MODEL FOR ASSESSING COMMERCIAL POTENTIAL:

1. Unmet need.
2. Prevalence of condition.
3. Ability to self-identify.
4. Regulatory feasibility.
5. Clinical studies required.
6. Competition/Alternatives.
7. Level of satisfaction/efficacy of existing treatments.
8. Safety/Side Effects.
9. Fit with existing business.
10. Market Size.
11. Likely erosion to Rx.
12. Degree of innovation.
13. Investment required.
14. Availability of drug.
15. Timeline.

Rather than chasing the sales line for a switch, I think that a change of approach is required. In the early stages, focus should be on whether the product can actually be sold OTC and to work out the methodology on how to scale this up successfully.

Switch involves grass roots marketing and building relationships with health professionals, pharmacists and consumers to facilitate behaviour change. Increased chances of success come with understanding the levers and drivers of such behaviour change and the passage of time.

It is ludicrous that the self care industry - with all its talent and resources - has recently been unable to make blockbuster drugs that have been prescribed successfully into self care versions. I don't think we are doing it right and I see the same mistakes being made over and over by companies working in isolation with limited in-house experience of switch.

TESTING

EARLY STAGE SWITCH TESTING

i.   Work out if you can actually sell it as a self care product.
ii.   Know how people decide to self-treat with it.
iii. Understand when people will come back to buy again.
iv.   Work out the consumer journey when they need advice.
v.   Find out how properly to engage pharmacists.
vi.   Establish the criteria to make it scalable.

POSITIONING

Getting the positioning right begins at the outset of the project. This is crucial. The process of evolving positioning involves marketing, medics, scientists, pharmacists, key opinion leaders, patient representatives and regulatory and it is a good idea to get expert help on this to get ultimate clarity.

- What is it?
- Who is this for?
- What does it do?
- Why and when should they use it?
- What is it going to be called?
- How does the potential user decide that they are suitable for the product?
- How does a pharmacist recognise them?
- What are the steps in their journey?
- How does the product communicate and interact with the lifestyle of the consumer?

Once this is worked out, it is a good idea to work up the label copy from a consumer perspective (rather than a regulatory one) and visual identity, including the brand name. Decide what you really want to say to the consumer and then overlay that with the regulatory speak and set format for labelling, according to the labelling regulations. It is a good idea to check early on whether it will all fit on the packaging. Some companies validate the positioning concepts at this stage through consumer research. You will also need to talk to an Intellectual Property Lawyer at this time to make sure that the trademarks, URLs and branding can be secured and set up in the right way.

DEAL BREAKERS

In the first stage of switch planning it is also a really good idea to try to define the deal breakers, ie the things that would be unacceptable restrictions or criteria and consequence of the reclassified product that may be proposed by the regulator. This could be restricted pack size, a lower dose, an age limit or a test and are usually criteria that could undermine the prescription setting, add significant cost or healthcare professionals current practice or things that simply just won't work.

"So maybe for switches a new approach is required that moves away from big-launch, high-sales models and considers an evolutionary approach, which establish a bond between consumer and product and harnesses emerging technology to reach people in a more intimate way than ever before."

Anna Maxwell

Chapter 9

CAN WE SWITCH IT?

SUMMARY

This section deals with the detailed assessment of the feasiblilty of a switch from the regulatory and commercial perspective and gives an overview of the regulatory process.

This chapter considers:-

1. How to prepare for an initial meeting with the regulatory body.

2. Working out the answers to the questions that might be raised yourselves.

3. Being aware of the limitations of commercial forecasting models that are designed to predict the future.

4. Why the industry should move away from high-spend, high sales-driven switch models and focus on slower-burn evolutionary models instead.

5. Planning the Risk Management Plan early in the process.

6. Being prepared for Public Consultation.

7. Thinking about innovation and developing the next generation of product.

MARKET RESEARCH

The first piece of market research is to obtain a meeting to discuss your switch options with the regulatory authority - I wouldn't spend a cent on any other market research or detailed financial modelling until an initial meeting has been held with the regulatory authority and their input sought on the proposed direction for the switch or the options. This can establish likely feasibility and identify any obstacles before any significant investment is made. It is also a good idea to get the views up front from the regulator so that the switch can be designed to overcome any obstacles that may present.

A Scientific Advice Meeting (SAM) can be requested in the UK via the MHRA website.[23] and these are always extremely valuable and considered as an essential part of the process. There is a fee payable for such meetings and in order to get the best value from the meeting it is vital to prepare for it. It is worth hiring external switch expertise to prepare for this if no one has done a SAM before; even if they have, an external perspective will deliver a better result. Sometimes companies run these themselves but they can be successfully managed and run by a third party if the company wants a light touch or to distance themselves from the discussions.

Unfortunately, politics can get in the way at this stage and slow things down. Sometimes the company has a critical project in a crucial stage of the regulatory process which means that regulatory group may be reluctant to have this kind of a meeting for fear that it has some impact on their other projects. Is this reality? The SAM is a non-binding advice meeting offered to facilitate the process of switching medicines, something that the regulator thinks is a good idea. The newly published MHRA process allows for a preliminary SAM (PSAM) that takes place before a SAM. If your regulatory authority doesn't have this type of forum, then demand one. Treat this meeting as market research with a group of the most important stakeholders – their advice is important.

PREPARING FOR SAM

SAM meetings are time-bound and are in a question-and-answer format. Two weeks prior to the meeting, the company is expected to provide rationale and background as to what is to be discussed so that the authority can gather the right heads in the room on the day or take soundings from and ask the right questions of the associated working groups and committees involved.

"BUT you also have to have worked out the answers yourselves so that you know how to shape the discussions,"

This means you have to prepare questions for them BUT you also have to have worked out the answers yourselves so that you know how to shape the discussions, especially when something is left of field. Also, it is important to understand in advance what the deal breakers would be, eg some kind of test that in theory could be easily done but in a pharmacy setting would be totally impossible, or something that would undermine the prescription setting. Decide whom you are going to take with you on the day and rehearse them, but keep the numbers down.

I have heard some company executives say that they have not found these types of meeting useful but that has never been my experience because of my approach to planning them. It is very important to prepare well and rehearse for these meetings to ensure that the team gets the most out of the exchange. Find out which MHRA disciplines will be represented at your meeting, eg Scientific Assessor, Medical Assessor, Risk Management Assessor.

It is important for the core team to spend time going through the detail together well in advance, and to set time aside for rehearsing beforehand. You will get out of these meetings what you put in. Meeting international colleagues, who have just arrived by plane, for the first time, an hour before the meeting starts, is a recipe for disaster. My mantra is "poor planning makes poor performance"... what more can I say?

> "poor planning makes poor performance"

THE NUMBERS

I have spent hundreds of my precious hours looking at spreadsheets that attempt to predict the future...and there are lots of companies who will take your money to come up with the answers for you with their magic boxes, theories and crystal balls! Usually these are best estimates based on what has been done or what has gone before. It is really hard (if not impossible) to predict what is going to happen with something that is completely new. Wake up! You are making an educated guess, it is not real, and it is based on assumptions on what might happen. But as no one knows for sure – just like the English weather forecast – most are likely to be just plain wrong!

The reason that organisations require this detail is because it helps plan resources, which is vital and helps validate the decision-making. However this type of data gets used as a "no-blame shield" for when things go wrong. The corporate mantra goes something like this:-

"we did this research that cost a lot of money so it must have been good and we made this really detailed forecasting model which said the sales would be this and we should spend that. So we did that, together with this and that too and now it hasn't worked. Sorry it is not my fault I did my best. We built a great model "

How liberating would it be just get on with it in the interests of public health? Find the self care solution that is scalable and ultimately makes return on investment through prototyping in the market place, ie through testing the methodology for real. Maybe it is not the drug that generates the profit but the service around it - a wellbeing programme, for example - and the medicine is simply part of that package.

In my view, if money is going to be spent at all, then it should be spent on prototyping, simulating reality or real-life testing in a controlled setting. This is the only way to get a handle on what might happen yet, even so, in the real world life is unpredictable.

When Nicorette switched in 1991, would anyone have built into their sales projections the impact of the shift in government policy on the sales, let alone the change in public attitude that has changed smoking from being mainstream to socially unacceptable? If they had, would they have been able to predict the size and scale of the market? Probably not.

"It is about changing a person who would normally rely on a doctor to tell them what to do into an individual who is competent and able to make the right decisions about their own self-treatment.

Although it will take time, such change is possible."

Part of the problem here is that there is a perception that switches require heavy investment up front which is true if the sales expectations are set very high in the first place and this has been historically the case. There are also entrenched marketing models employed for brands that require certain thresholds of awareness to be reached, prevalence and a whole host of other factors.

It takes a lot of boxes of product to pay for a £5m world-changing TV campaign - if your ex factory price is £2.50 and RRP £6.00 this equates to about 3 million packs. How many brands achieve these volumes from a standing start? Depressingly, not many in the self care arena.

So maybe for switches a new approach is required that moves away from big-launch, high-sales models and considers an evolutionary approach, which establish a bond between consumer and product and harnesses emerging technology to reach people in a more intimate way than ever before. After all, this is a journey. It is about changing a person who would normally rely on a doctor to tell them what to do into an individual who is competent and able to make the right decisions about their own self-treatment.

Although it will take time, such change is possible.

THE REGULATORY PROCESS

This is well documented. Recently established guidelines for the UK process can be found at the MHRA website www.mhra.gov.uk [13]. It is a good idea to familiarise yourself and core team members with this overview as it explains the steps and what needs to be done to meet the requirements of the regulator. Other countries in Europe base their switch programmes on a similar process.

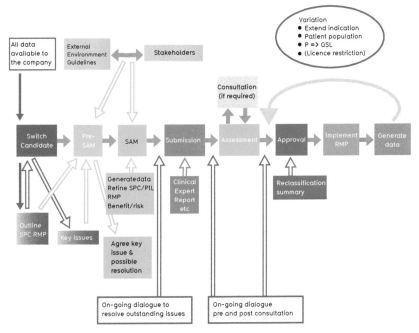

How to change the legal classification of a medicine in the UK
Reproduced with kind permission from PAGB.

RISK MANAGEMENT PLANNING

Consideration of a Risk Management Plan (RMP) is essential to every switch. The RMP gives an indication to MHRA of how the company will manage any of the risks associated with reclassification. For less complex switches or in cases where there are few/minor risks, the RMP may just include something about labelling, for example. The RMP should be submitted as part of the reclassification application and is seen as a critical part of it since it now should include the pharmacy protocol as part of the risk minimisation activities. For more complex switches or situations where there are specific risks, there may be a requirement for additional measures.

Companies should start thinking about the RMP with their regulatory strategy as early as possible. The benefit: risk Value Tree Framework[34] is very helpful in clarifying the core issues that form consideration in the Risk Management Plan.

THE PUBLIC CONSULTATION

This is the part of the regulatory process where details of the switch are put into the public domain so that public input can be gained and there is a flow of information and opinion exchange. Not every switch is consulted upon; the decision to consult depends upon the regulator. A Public Consultation can cause debate and comment which is not always supportive or positive so my advice is to prepare for Public Consultation as if it were a Crisis Management situation. That way, the bases are covered and you are prepared.

INNOVATION

As mentioned previously, it is a good idea to also think about innovation up front and what the pipeline is going to look like to support your switch in the future, eg new formats, different strengths, other indications, line extensions and whether there is a further step in the switch process that you would like to explore, such as P to GSL. If P to GSL is the intention, then this is something that should be discussed at a Scientific Advice Meeting with the regulatory body and the thinking built in to the switch planning at this stage.

To minimise the time for the transition, data can be collected from the point the product becomes available in market but this needs to be set up right at the outset to support the regulatory needs and could be part of a Risk Management Plan (RMP). Most companies don't think about this until midway through the project – I encourage everyone to think about it much earlier on.

"A stakeholder is a person or body who could influence the outcome of your switch..."

Anna Maxwell

Chapter 10

UNDERSTANDING STAKEHOLDERS

This chapter highlights the importance of stakeholders throughout the switch process.

1. There are internal and external stakeholders.

2. Stakeholders need to be identified and engaged early in the process.

3. It is desirable to create a long-term, two-way relationship that continues through the planning process and long after implementation.

4. There are 5 types of external stakeholder.
    a. The Regulatory Body.
    b. Key Opinion Leaders.
    c. The interested.
    d. Your customers.
    e. The media.

5. You need a Stakeholder Strategy and a Stakeholder Contact Plan.

6. Having consistent key messages is vital for each target audience.

7. Not everyone will support what you are doing.

8. The switch must work for your customers otherwise they won't be able to implement it.

9. No plan survives contact with the enemy, so build as much 20:20 foresight as you can.

UNDERSTANDING STAKEHOLDERS

Stakeholders are those individuals or organisations that have an influence on your switch. Some stakeholders are directly involved with the project and others indirectly involved, but all have varying degrees of influence.

Identifying stakeholders is important. These are the organisations - they may be charities or self-help groups, or individuals such as Key Opinion Leaders, professional bodies or expert medical groups - who could influence your switch positively or negatively. Getting them on board early or at least understanding their position on your switch can provide useful insight into the hurdles and obstacles that you may encounter further down the line.

A switch tends to be high profile in any organisation; there are internal stakeholders as well as external stakeholders and they need to be managed through the process through planned communication around realistic goals. Proactive management of the internal stakeholders (see diagram) has a significant impact in keeping up momentum and morale throughout the planning and implementations stages. They are just as important as the external stakeholders.

Internal stakeholders are those that the core team may have to engage with to get work done in order to bring the launch to market or perhaps influence to achieve commercial goals or an investment. These would typically include the following disciplines in a large organisation and will be brought in by the core project team when needed, as they are involved at a particular stage of the process but not engaged all the time.

Nevertheless, they need to be aware of their roles and likely timescales for their involvement so that thy can plan their workload. It is no good sending copy for approval just as the legal signatory is about to jet off on holiday for two weeks.

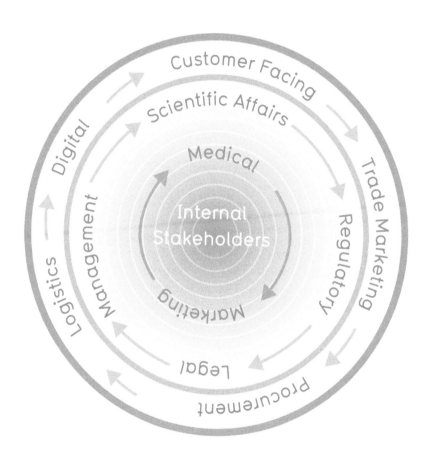

Senior management are key stakeholders that have to be managed proactively as they are some of the most important stakeholders in the equation. We talked earlier about communication and the management of their expectations. It is key to keep the mood positive, demonstrate progress and highlight the wins, however small, as this keeps up the momentum. Within any organisation there will be detractors as well as supporters and working out who they are and allowing the time to listen to their views is a good idea so that you can come up with plans that are better and neutralise any concerns where possible.

CONCERNS

The types of concerns that are likely to come up are as follows: -

- How to overcome potential erosion to prescriptions.
- Fit with the public health agenda.
- Fit with existing prescribing algorithms.
- Getting doctors or dentists to buy in to the concept.
- Not upsetting doctors.
- How to educate pharmacists to a level of competence about the condition or category.
- How effectively to allow doctors and other healthcare professionals know about the switch without confusing them.
- Pharmacy hopping.
- Side effects and red flag scenarios – what might be missed.
- The numbers.

External stakeholders can make or break a switch and, where possible, these groups or individuals need to be brought on side so they can be supportive through the regulatory transition or at least close enough you can understand their point of view. Stakeholders come in all shapes and sizes. They can be key opinion leaders, experts in their field, professional bodies, public awareness groups, Facebook forums, charities, customers and competitors... there is a whole raft of possibilities.

Some stakeholders are critical to the switch process and other have less influence. By listening to their views and opinions during the switch process they too can help shape the design and outcome to create a better solution for self care.

The largest stakeholder of all is the Regulatory Authority where due process must be followed and it is best to have people on the team who understand putting switch applications in, working peer to peer with the regulatory body. People who know about switches understand the process, language and method of working and can work to facilitate the needs of the authority quickly and expediently.

Apart from the regulatory authority there are four other types of stakeholder: -

Key Opinion Leaders. (KOLs) who are part of the positioning and regulatory process - a key element of the core team. They help deliver the rationale, provide input for the expert reports, and should be prepared to promote and defend the switch and arguments all along the way. They are ideally advocates with a strong positive reputation in the relevant field either from a clinical or scientific perspective. It is helpful if they have access to research and academia.

The Interested. There is a much wider universe of people or groups who may have influence or interest by virtues of their own mission such as the professions, government departments like the Department of Health, public awareness groups, patient forums, bloggers, pressure groups, competition etc. Part of the planning process is to identify these groups, prepare a list, and prioritise them according to their likely attitude and level of influence and then work up a plan to communicate with them if and when appropriate.

Your Customers. It is wise to talk early on to the Pharmacy Superintendents of key customers to establish their support for the switch, especially if it is going to involve the development of some kind of service. There is a lot of commercial sensitivity around this - when is the right time to talk to a large pharmacy retailer? On the one hand, the retailers are partners in building the market but with their own-label portfolios they are also competitors – so some kind of truce needs to be drawn up here to get switches right. Brand owners do not want discussions to de-generate into an own-label discussion from the start, as has happened in the past.

"The switch has to be designed so that it works for your customers otherwise they won't be able to implement it the way you planned."

Early conversations at the retailer level can give useful practical perspective on the switch concept and can help shape how it would actually work in practice in the retail scenario. It is important to work out the counselling and sales pathway - from the front line pharmacy counter assistant to the pharmacist's consultation, intervention or approval. There are other considerations too. The obvious one is determining and setting up any training that may be required but don't forget to give consideration to ensure continuity of supply on the dispensing business and to minimise the risk of confusion at launch and emergence of unforeseen consequences. The switch has to be designed so that it works for your customers otherwise they won't be able to implement it the way you planned.

Although the domain of the customer-facing activity is the sales or commercial team, I strongly recommend that the project leader for the switch is present at the meetings so that any nuances and opportunities can be picked up and explored at the time. If these meetings are held early enough in the process then ideas and enhancements can be incorporated into the design of the switch. Meetings of this nature should be undertaken under confidentiality agreements.

Working out who the buyer is for your switch in the different channels and customer groups can be interesting and is sometimes left until very late in the process. It can sometimes throw up challenges in that new relationships may have to be built.

The media Harnessing the media has powerful consequences but it has to be done at the right time in the process to avoid breaking any rules on advertising and promotion of the prescription product or indeed the new switch variant. It is fine to talk to the press once the project is in the public domain, ie at the time of Public Consultation, should there be one.
The pharmacy trade press generally get excited about switches – use this enthusiasm wisely, it is the start of your marketing campaign, although, just as with any communication, the messages need to be carefully prepared. Concentrate on the sound bites that will harness support for the switch with pharmacists and have ways of dealing with any negatives to diffuse that focus.

It is rare in these early stages that the consumer press pick up on switch stories, unless they are of sensational interest, eg Viagra or Alli. However, it is worth communicating some key messages to titles at this time just in case there is a space on their health pages - particularly if there is a major public health need that your switch is addressing. Again this starts the seeding process in the mind of the consumer and every little sound bite and byline helps.

All external stakeholders should be managed through the process so that they ideally are supportive of the switch or at least hold a neutral position. Of course, not every organisation is going to be supportive so through a process of identifying who the different stakeholders are it is possible to work out advocates and detractors.

By developing intelligence and in some cases starting a dialogue with them in advance their likely position can be worked out to establish whether they are either supportive, negative or neutral. Once their position is understood, they can be proactively managed with planned communication and messaging if required.

But stakeholder management is not just about a one-off meeting, a letter or phone call. Instead, it is about building a relationship and a supportive network, some face to face, some arm's length and making sure that these people are kept in the loop throughout the process and beyond.

Why have a stakeholder management plan?

> The goal is to get as many stakeholders as possible at the time of public consultation (if there is one) to write positively to MHRA in support of the switch.

A stakeholder management plan:-

- Enables the core team to identify stakeholders with an interest in the switch, whether from a positive or negative standpoint.

- Helps view the switch from an external perspective and draw out any concerns or negatives and prepare for them.

- Provides the framework for a stakeholder communication programme that will employ strategies to manage/engage each group according to their priority through the public consultation to launch and beyond.

- Helps identify specific resource required to manage this key communications element of the switch process.

What is the stakeholder management plan for?

- To lobby stakeholder organisations with the rationale for the switch.

- Encourage stakeholders to respond to the public consultation by providing them with strong key messages that they can "cut and paste" or interpret in their own words.

- Gauge reactions from interested parties and avoid surprises.

- Be prepared to deal with negative PR at public consultation and be in a position to neutralise it.

STAKEHOLDER CONTACT STRATEGY

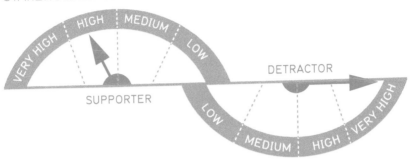

Stakeholder Degree of Influence	BRIEFING METHOD	
	SUPPORTER	DETRACTOR
Very High	F2f Meeting	Prepare Q&A Brief KOL Monitor
High	Telecom + Follow up Email	Prepare Q&A Monitor
Medium	Briefing Letter	Prepare Q&A Monitor
Low	Press Release to Relevant Titles	Prepare Q&A Monitor

As part of your switch implementation programme to support the regulatory process you need to draw up a stakeholder management plan. This will identify and map the different stakeholders and group them in terms of the degree of influence or relative importance they have to the switch or your business. The plan is then prioritised to form an actionable contact plan.

Obviously you cannot contact everybody face to face, so different methods of communication need to be employed to get the message across in the way you want.

As part of this planning it is vital to decide what you are consistently going to say to each group and work up the key messages, learning them so that they can become verbatim. What do you want these people to remember? What's in it for them? How do you want them to represent your switch within their organisation? It is very easy to get carried away, especially in face-to-face meetings, and tell them about all the challenges and hurdles and then that becomes the message that these people remember and transfer. Avoid this by having an approved set of messages for each target audience.

Anyone who is involved with the stakeholder contact plan should fully understand the rationale for the switch and be well rehearsed in the key messages. Their role is also to gather intelligence and feedback reactions and feed these back to the core project team.

Be familiar with the potential objections, have answers, rehearse them and know how to deal with them.

Dealing with negative stakeholders

There are two types of negative stakeholders: -

- Those you know about.
- Those who surprise you with a response that is different to what you had anticipated.

There will be always negative stakeholders, for example in the case of the switch of trimethoprim where the microbiologist lobby came out in force at the public consultation. So be prepared for the scenario that not everyone will agree with the switch or the way it is proposed. However, the fact that you know up front that there will be some negativity is good because it means that you can work out their likely objections and use this to base your measured and well-prepared responses. This means you are prepared for the surprises when they come unannounced. Whether you decide to tackle the known negative stakeholders head on is a matter for the stakeholder management plan to address through the prioritisation process. However, in my experience, the best way to deal with them is to prepare a robust Question & Answer Document (Q&A) that is approved in advance and can be issued as needed when any flak starts to fly. Having KOLs trained and on standby to deal with issues as they arise is also a good idea, even fielding them in the media if needs be.

The professional bodies representing doctors such as the BMA and the Royal College of General Practitioners are important stakeholders to communicate with regarding switch. Ideally these communications are best managed face to face but don't necessarily expect a positive response. Instead, be prepared to have an open discussion with them on a peer-to-peer basis. It is a good idea to take a respected key opinion leader along with you when you meet with them.

KEY STAKEHOLDER MESSAGES

These are different to advertising messages as they are a summary of the rationale for the switch addressed to the various target audiences that you will encounter. They may have a core theme with slight modifications depending on which of these audiences you're talking to. For example, a pharmacist key message may have the same sentiment as one for a key opinion leader but the wording may be different to reflect the needs of the different recipient.

The regulator, on the other hand, is interested in key messages around improving public health, widening access and increasing choice, whereas a body representing the medical profession may need to be more reassured about risk/benefit elements of the switch and a pharmacist about how it is likely to enhance their role.

You can never guarantee what anyone is going to say on the day – so if there are really important messages that you want to get across to deliver your arguments then use technology to do so – film it or write it down. The benefits of this approach are that you can craft your message in advance and capture it in the way that it was intended rather than leaving it to chance. It is really inexpensive to do this now - you don't even need a professional film crew if you are short of cash. Just a smartphone, a wonder teen and a clever app.

STAKEHOLDER MANAGEMENT – TO DO LIST

- Draw up a list of stakeholders that impact your switch.
- Prioritise them according to degree of influence and importance to your business/switch.
- Produce a contact plan of how you are going to communicate.
- Allocate resources.
- Get out there and communicate.
- Record feedback formally and review responses.
- Act upon the feedback in shaping your plans.
- Continue the dialogue and keep the stakeholder informed.
- Build 20:20 foresight.

BUILDING 20:20 FORESIGHT

No plan, however well thought through, survives contact with the enemy and it is quite amazing how, once the product gets to market, everyone around becomes an expert on the flaws and what could have been done better or differently. After launch, snide remarks such as *"I knew that wouldn't work"* or *"I knew that would happen"* become the coffee-machine conversations, especially if you are chasing the sales line in the first few months and it can be quite isolating. It can actually be much worse than that: when you present your plans to all and sundry during the process of getting the switch switched, there will be people who whisper at the back of the room who are full of ideas as to why it is not going to work. Unfortunately, they don't speak up for fear of being called negative. Such views are really valuable and rather than wait to hear it in hindsight there needs to be a forum in which these negatives can be captured and harnessed during the planning to create a better-designed switch plan prior to locking everything down into implementation.

My advice is to gather a group of internal and external stakeholders to walk though the plan with the sole purpose of challenging it to come up with something better – build at least one 20:20 foresight intelligence gathering session into your switch plan. Go ahead and smash it all to bits!

Things that can go wrong with stakeholders:

- KOL jumps ship.
- KOL hijacks your cause for their own.
- Interview with the press concentrates on all the negatives.
- The regulatory authorities come back with a deal breaker.
- There is a leak

THE LAST WORD

There are lots of people involved in a switch across an organisation and managing their expectations is key to driving momentum, keeping focused and getting results. Like preparing a team for the Olympics, focus, preparation mindset, motivation and morale are important drivers for the project, especially during the regulatory assessment and negotiation phase.

Some internal stakeholders may be interested in your success because it impacts their own role in the business; some because they are going to have to pick up the ball at some time and others because what you are working on is an exciting game changer and really interesting.

Others may try to block it because they are perhaps risk averse or are considering what they think are better commercial opportunities, such as emerging markets. There will be some who can't see past the obvious hurdles; others who think that the cost is too much or the risk is too great. One thing that you can be sure of is that your switch project will receive a lot of attention because growth is automatically assumed and part of the equation, the stakes are high and there are reputations to consider.

A switch is not always guaranteed to come to fruition. Companies tend to assume that it they decide to switch a molecule then it will definitely happen and pretty soon expectations and launch dates become the topic of conversation and anticipation and pressure begins to build. Yet the regulatory process is out of your control and there can sometimes be quite a lot of negotiation with the authorities on certain aspects of the switch which causes delay. Remember that this a normal part of the process. It may be that the authorities ask you to provide further rationale or clinical studies in support of the process, all of which impact both the timeline and cost.

The other consideration to bear in mind is that once the regulatory process has run its course, the switch may look a little different to what was submitted in the first place. If this happens, it is important to reflect on what has been agreed and modify any plans accordingly. For example, if 7.5% of your prevalence is in the 40-45 age group and the regulator decides the age criteria to be 45 years upwards then any sales assumption needs to be adjusted to take account of this.

It may be that what you end up with does not meet the early aims and objectives for the project and so a final step in the process should be a reality check to see where you have ended up.

Exercise caution about committing to launch timings until you are well into the regulatory process and at least past the first post in term of the first request for information. It is very easy for projects to begin to slip and every day that is lost just adds another day on to the timeline. You need to manage the timeline closely as well as expectations and hold people to account on the deliverables. If the project starts to slip then enthusiasm and support for the project can begin to ebb away and this can impact perception of your skills as a project leader.

The way to avoid this is to set up regular communication and input sessions with the various internal stakeholders. Make sure that they are working to a plan and that meetings are agenda-led and action-oriented, then follow meetings up with action-focused minutes that hold people accountable in terms of deliverables and timelines. Share ideas and get the key players involved early on, let them know what is expected of them and when they will need to be involved.

There are bound to be setbacks along the way and you can harness the power of the team to get through these. You need to develop a culture of infectious enthusiasm that pervades your organisation: this will automatically keep morale high and problems will solve themselves. Make it fun to be part of the switch team.

AND, FINALLY, REMEMBER THESE FIVE INSIGHTS

1. Every switch is unique.
2. Focus on the public health benefits.
3. Commit resource, pay attention to detail and allocate proper time with injections of switch expertise from people who know about switch to help switches projects thrive.
4. Persuade your business to commit at least three years investment up front for the project, win or lose.
5. Consider the whole mix, ie both direct and indirect effects, when evaluating success.

Good luck!

"In the last 30 years there have been 143 switches in the UK and only 11 could be said to have not met expectation which is a 92.5% success rate. Taking the last 10 years the success rate is 61% which seem like favourable odds considering 9 out of 10 UK businesses fail in the first 5 years of trading."

Anna Maxwell

Chapter 11

WHY THESE SWITCHES WORKED

This is my take on the following switches and why they were successful based on my observations over time. For more examples please go to www.dynamicswitch.co.uk

Summary

Loperamide – Imodium. Date: 1983

Janssen's philosophy was to build brands through pharmacy education and public relations as there was limited advertising in the early stages of any product's launch over the counter.

Nurofen. Date: 1983

Nurofen is the OTC version of the blockbuster drug Brufen that was patented in 1962 and marketed by Boots Pharmaceuticals enjoying success as Advil in the USA in a co-marketing agreement with Wyeth.

Chloramphenicol. Date: 2005

This drug is regularly held up as a great example of a switch, but it was a dead cert right from the start.

Acyclovir. Date: 1993

Like Chloramphenicol, Acyclovir is another example of switch where pharmacists were already sending consumers presenting with cold sore symptoms to their GP to get a prescription for Zovirax, so success was inevitable.

Levonorgestrel – Morning After Pill. Date: 2001

In my view Levonelle is one of the best examples of switch in recent times. The category of emergency hormonal contraception was a revolutionary new category for over-the-counter medicine and the topic highly controversial because of the ethical and moral implications.

LOPERAMIDE – IMODIUM
Date: 1983

Janssen's philosophy was to build brands through pharmacy education and public relations as there was limited advertising in the early stages of any product's launch over the counter. Initially GP representatives called on pharmacies in the afternoons to sell Imodium. From around 1985 the company fielded a dedicated sales team who were trained in the same way as pharmaceutical territory managers with a strong ethical and training bias to their mission.

The symptoms of diarrhoea are acute and easily recognisable: it is highly inconvenient for the sufferer who wants to get back to normal as soon as possible, and is both a physical and emotional experience.

The drug is highly effective and works fast, with results usually seen with the first dose. A 4 pack and an 8 pack were launched but pharmacists were unconvinced about the number of doses in the 4-pack version and this failed[12]. The relatively expensive 8 pack became the recommended pack of choice. However, the price was at a significant premium to the competition with the NHS prescription charge depressing the off take.

Imodium was not advertised to the general public in the early years of its OTC status. This was due to concern that NHS reimbursement may be lost if the product was advertised to consumers whilst still being available on NHS prescription. Back in 1983, pharmacists were resistant to change and reluctant to recommend and sell products that had been previously available on prescription. So rates of uptake were organic rather than a step change, which is what would have been expected with such a major innovation.

There was also some resistance to the switch of Imodium because of a pervading clinical view that it was better to flush out whatever was causing the problem with oral rehydration sachets such as Dioralyte.

In 1985, Janssen adopted a dual-branding approach and the company launched Arret, a rebranded consumer version of loperamide that could be promoted to consumers through advertising. Arret's marketing was targeted at the holiday-maker so broadening its use to be purchased as a preventive measure. This was initially successful, supported by seasonal advertising; the different brand name and pricing strategy meant that prescriptions were still filled with Imodium. Arret enjoyed success during the holiday season.

Kaolin-and-morphine-based remedies were the major competition at the time, as they were cheap and the first choice for recommendation. As time progressed, however, abuse problems with the liquid versions of these medicines began to impact pharmacists' support for them. Gradually, Imodium and Arret got a toehold in pharmacist recommendation and Boots introduced their own label, Diareze.

Critical success factors for loperamide

- The inconvenience of the condition.
- Symptoms easily recognisable by the consumer.
- Emergency use – need it now.
- Self-limiting condition.
- Next Generation. Highly effective, fast-acting product.
- Medicine cabinet item "Just in case."
- Detailing force visiting pharmacy for peer-to-peer discussion.
- Rx heritage.
- Inferior Competition.
- Additional travel positioning.

IBUPROFEN – NUROFEN
Date: 1983

Nurofen is the OTC version of the blockbuster drug Brufen that was patented in 1962 and marketed by Boots Pharmaceuticals enjoying success as Advil in the USA in a co-marketing agreement with Wyeth.

Nurofen was launched over the counter in 1983 (30 years ago) by Crookes Healthcare, the OTC sales and marketing vehicle in the UK that enabled the Boots company to distribute brands such as Optrex, Strepsils and Cream E45 to the independent pharmacy universe in the UK outside the Boots the Chemist chain. At the time, Boots had approximately 1000 stores and the majority of the UK's female population shopped at Boots at least once a month.

As a Boots-owned product and a P medicine, Nurofen received unparalleled support from Boots stores, occupying prime position on the chemist counter top displays and window displays. Staff training included a road show that visited major cities to promote the product alongside Cream E45. Boots pharmacy staff were encouraged to recommend Boots brands where possible and Nurofen fell under the umbrella of a Boots brand so began to enjoy the benefits of Boots Pharmacist and Pharmacy staff recommendation as first line.

I don't think any brand could afford to buy the level of support that was secured by Crookes for Nurofen back then. Move the clock forward to today and the promotional fees would be too expensive to obtain that kind of exposure and engagement. The major competitors at the time were Anadin (aspirin) owned by Whitehall Labs, a subsidiary of Wyeth who were so successful in the US with Advil, and also Boots Paracetamol 100's, a generic in a brown glass bottle with cotton wool wadding and a cap at 99p.

It is important to point out that in pharmacies at this time there was limited self-selection and major categories such as cough cold and pain relief were stocked behind the chemist counter or physically displayed on it. Medicines were, in the main, requested. It was in the early 1990s that a wider selection of cough and cold remedies and analgesics were made available for self-selection as Superdrug began to erode share from Boots.

Nurofen was supported with print and TV advertising in its early years and in 1990 there was a step change as Nurofen was advertised with a new ground-breaking advertisement[26] that used the sound track from Pink Floyd's Great Gig In the sky. This is the campaign that established the brand. Sales of Nurofen in 1994 were around £18m and the launch of Nurofen Plus[27] (ibuprofen + codeine) in 1995 took sales over the £20m mark.

In the early 1990s, McNeil (Johnson & Johnson) tried and failed to launch a competitor to Nurofen called Inoven which was a caplet (not tablet) in a novel flip-top box. From memory, it was targeted as a back pain product with an advertisement that had butterflies floating over the affected areas. It had to be the most consumer-researched product launch that I ever saw in my time as a Boots buyer – I listed it as I thought it could fly. What McNeil could not have predicted was the strength of the uprising from Crookes Healthcare team on the ground who seemingly did not allow Inoven to take root anywhere in the independent trade. I don't know how they did it, but I do know that the product has been consigned to the annals of history affectionately known as "in the bin", so maybe there is a clue here?

There was a paradigm shift in 1993 when entrepreneurial company Galpharm surprised the market by achieving the switch of ibuprofen from pharmacy-only status to general sales list. This meant that Galpharm in collaboration with Wallis Laboratories - not Crookes, with the mighty Boots backing - could lead the march and take ibuprofen into the grocery channel, offering the supermarkets own-label ibuprofen that could compete with Boots.

In 1995, as a result of this generic competition, Nurofen's share started to slide. This stimulated a programme of innovation that saw the introduction of line extensions, new actives and different formats. Around this time there was another threat to Nurofen's position and that was a decision by Boots to put all general sales list medicines out for self-selection so that they could better compete with Superdrug and the grocers like Asda and Tesco who were beginning to take an interest in the self-medication categories.

This change in market dynamics hit Nurofen hard because it was stocked behind the chemist counter as a P product and not available for self-selection. Although the brand did continue to grow, the pace of growth was slowed by this sea change because the footfall at the chemist counter dropped in favour of self-selection areas, also resulting in fewer healthcare conversations in pharmacy.

The other contributory factor in the mix was Retail Price Maintenance (RPM), which applied to all branded medicines in that they had to be sold at the same price in all outlets by law. This was abolished in 1999 in a move stimulated by Asda. However, this had significance for Nurofen and Galpharm's own-label ibuprofen introduction because the Galpharm product was outside the scope of RPM and with "free" pricing could be offered to the consumer at a much cheaper price. Boots had actually been undercutting branded products with their own label for years, thus getting round the RPM legislation. Now the tables had turned: no longer did they have control over the ibuprofen market. Eventually after two years, Crookes switched a 200mg version of Nurofen and took it GSL in 1996, and the original P variant was discontinued in 2002.

It is the combination of the switch, the intervention of an entrepreneur and the continuous stream of innovation and economic change that has built Nurofen in regular increments each year over time into the brand that it is today, but it has taken 30 years to get there.

Early critical success factors for ibuprofen

- High prevalence of pain in the population.
- Next-generation molecule.
- Superior safety profile to aspirin.
- Rx heritage.
- Boots support and exposure.
- Footfall at the chemist counter.

Later critical success factors for Nurofen

- Generic competition.
- Innovation and line extension.
- Advertising and promotion.
- Time.

CHLORAMPHENICOL
Date: 2005

This drug is regularly held up as a great example of a switch, but it was a dead cert right from the start. As a pharmacist, I found it frustrating when a customer presented with a gunky eye perfectly describing their symptoms on waking and all I could do was to send them to the doctor to obtain a prescription only for them to return (or not) a few hours later, having walked around with their contagious condition for hours longer than then needed to.

That is the perfect example of a discrete set of symptoms easily recognisable by the patient, yet pharmacists were regularly sending patients to the doctor to get a script. So Pharmacists were already primed, engaged and champing at the bit even before the switch success was inevitable.

It is a great example of how a switch can enhance the role of the pharmacist, save time and cost for the NHS and increase convenience for the customer, as well as minimising the spread of an infectious condition in the community.

Critical success factors for Chloramphenicol

- Easily recognisable symptoms.
- Pre-prepared pharmacists.
- It is compelling: you need to get it sorted out quickly.
- Contagious and spreads.

Acyclovir – Zovirax
DATE 1993

Like Chloramphenicol, Acyclovir is another example of switch where pharmacists were already sending consumers presenting with cold sore symptoms to their

GP to get a prescription for Zovirax, so success was inevitable. What is great about this switch is that through advertising and promotion Zovirax was able to promote the concept of treating the tingle to prevent the eruption happening in the first place - not so easy when you have to make an appointment to see your doctor first. This positioning reduced the level of suffering for the person concerned as with an OTC product you can prevent an eruption, thus opening up new possibilities for people to carry Zovirax in their bags as a rescue product that hopefully they didn't have to use. Zovirax Cream achieved GSL status in 2004.

Critical Success Factors for Zovirax

- Highly effective product – it really works.
- Pre-prepared pharmacists.
- Awareness of Zovirax as a prescription brand.
- Emotionally driven.
- Handbag essential.

LEVONORGESTREL – LEVONELLE MORNING AFTER PILL
Date:2001

In my view Levonelle is one of the best examples of switch in recent times. The category of emergency hormonal contraception was a revolutionary new category for over-the-counter medicine and the topic highly controversial because of the ethical and moral implications. Pharmacists were polarised into those who agreed with the principle and those who didn't. The Pharmaceutical Journal was full of letters every week discussing the subject, to stock or not to stock, and the moral dilemma that faced some because it was thought that Levonelle would encourage promiscuity amongst young women.

For the first time, the multiple retailers found themselves in a position where their employee pharmacists in some cases refused to stock the product and provide any kind of service at all. Religious establishments and the general public also had their views on the matter to throw into the melting pot. The debate rumbled on for a long time.

As a result of all this controversy and the attitudes of the various stakeholders, Schering Plough (now Bayer Schering) had to carefully plan the launch around these sensitivities to tread carefully and this drove the marketing team down a particular route. I am not sure whether this was by default or design. First of all, there was no big bang TV advertising campaign because pregnancy advisory services were not allowed to be advertised on TV until 2009. Levonelle was launched initially through a face-to-face tactical sales force detail. Not surprisingly, because of the controversy, the initial uptake was slow build and many pharmacists rejected the listings on moral grounds. One thing that is to be said about the professional and public reaction is that it created publicity for the launch above and beyond that which any marketing campaign could deliver and you couldn't really miss it.

Slowly listings were built in stores with pharmacists who were sympathetic to the opportunity and sales began to develop from a low base as Levonelle begun to be established on request. The marketing was quite soft sell – initially subtle and sensitively produced print ads that had the tone more of a public health initiative rather than a branded advertising campaign through posters and magazine ads.

However, in 2004 a not-so-subtle London Underground poster campaign, featuring the strapline "Immaculate Contraception" was withdrawn following complaints from Catholic groups.

Around 2006 in a bid to reduce pregnancy in the under-18 age group by 50% and to increase awareness of Sexually Transmitted Infection (STI) NHS Primary Care Trusts throughout the UK began to develop enhanced services for Emergency Hormonal Contraception under Patient Group Directive. This meant that for the first time and for certain people defined in the PGD pharmacists could consult and give Emergency Hormonal Contraception where appropriate with the bill for the drug and the consultation service being picked up by the NHS.

In April 2009, 8 years since the switch, an ad for Levonelle One Step showed a woman waking up next to her partner and then taking a trip to the pharmacy to ask for the pill, which is available without a prescription. It was broadcast after the 9pm watershed across a range of channels. This move still caused outrage amongst ProLife groups concerned still for young women who may be influenced by the advertising campaign.

Being highly sensitive to the likely reactions of certain factions of the population is paramount. A parallel for the launch can be drawn with crisis management initiative where numerous stakeholders had to be carefully managed to make the product a success.

Critical success factors for Levonorgestrol

- Sexual health category.
- Controversial.
- Stakeholder Management.
- Face-to-face training and detailing.
- Low-key marketing activity.
- Enhanced Pharmacy Services.
- Public Health Focus from NHS.
- Pharmacy Patient Group Directive (PGD)
  – pharmacists now get paid for providing an NHS service.
- Time.

For more examples of switches that worked and those that have not go to www.dynamicswitch.co.uk

Glossary

BPH	Benign Prostatic Hyperplasia (same as LUTS).
GSL	General Sales List Medicine.
IBS	Irritable Bowel Syndrome.
KOL	Key Opinion Leader.
LUTS	Lower Urinary Tract Symptoms (same as BPH).
MA	Marketing Authorisation /Licence.
MA Holder	Brand Owner/Owner of the MA.
MHRA	Medicines and Healthcare products Regulatory Agency (UK).
NHS	National Health Service (UK).
OTC	Over the Counter.
P	Pharmacy Only medicine.
POM	Prescription Only Medicine.
Rx	Prescription.
SAM	Scientific Advice Meeting.
SmPC	Summary of Product Characteristics.
TURPS	Transurethral resection of the prostate.
WWHAM	A mnemonic for assessing symptoms in pharmacy. Who for? What symptoms?: How long?; What action? Other medicines?

References

1   PAGB Get well, feel well & stay well A vision for Self Care in the United Kingdom

2   Symphony IRI Data 52 Weeks to December 2011 Retail Prices. Find the latest published UK market figures at http://www.pagb.co.uk/

3   Medicines, Medical Devices and the Law edited by John O'Grady, Ian Dobbs-Smith, Nigel Walsh, Michael Spencer

4   www.drchrissteele.com

5   Follow Tim @timberners_lee

6   http://www.nhs.uk/livewell/smoking/pages/stopsmokingnewhome.aspx#close, www.nicorette.co.uk/active-stop, www.quitmasters.co.uk, www.quitwithhelp.co.uk, http://smokefree.nhs.uk/quit-tools/quit-kit/

7   WHO Tobacco Dependence Treatment in England Martin Raw & Ann McNeill 2002

8   http://www.d2dlimited.com/

9   http://www.bbc.co.uk/health/physical_health/conditions/constipation1.shtml

10 http://www.tellyads.com/show_movie.php?filename=TA1787

11 http://www.guardian.co.uk/media/2007/apr/28/advertising.comment

13 25 Years of POM to P . Pharmacy Magazine Autumn 2008.

12 HOW TO CHANGE THE LEGAL CLASSIFICATION OF A MEDICINE IN THE UK.
    http://www.mhra.gov.uk/Howweregulate/Medicines/Licensingofmedicines/Legalstatusandreclassification/index.htm

14 Pharmacy Magazine July 2012

15 PCA Data England 2010 Pub 2011 & England 2011 Pub 2012 BNF Category 7.4.1.0

16 MHRA Estimate

17 http://eur-lex.europa.eu 31993L0042 Council Directive 93/42/EEC of 14 June 1993 concerning medical devices

18 EU Cosmetics Directive (76/768/EEC)

19 EU Food Supplements Directive 2002/46/EC

20 http://www.aesgp.eu/facts-figures/market-data/#pharma

21 HTTP://WWW.NHS.UK/NHSENGLAND/HEALTHCOSTS/PAGES/PRESCRIPTIONCOSTS.ASPX

22 http://www.zinc-ahead.com/

23 http://www.mhra.gov.uk/Howweregulate/Medicines/Licensingofmedicines/Informationforlicenceapplicants/Otherusefulservicesandinformation/Scientificadviceforlicenceapplicants/Requestforscientificadviceform/index.htm

24 'Improving the Decision-Making Process for Non-prescription Drugs: A Framework for Benefit-Risk Assessment' Brass et al Clin Pharmacol Ther 90:791 2011. An abstract is available at: www.nature.com/clpt/journal/v90/n6/full/clpt2011231a.html

25 http://en.wikipedia.org/wiki/Responsibility_assignment_matrix

26 http://www.youtube.com/watch?v=cbuFxxDIBWw

27 Symphony IRI published data

28 AESGP input to the European Commission's Study on the Availability of Medicinal Products for Human Use. July 2012

29 OTC Bulletin 30 November 2011

References

30 EUROPEAN COMMISSION VOLUME 2A: Procedures for marketing authorisation CHAPTER 1 MARKETING AUTHORISATION November 2005

31 www.northwest.nhs.uk

32 http://shortreports.rsmjournals.com/content/2/7/56.full

33 Racks of Make up and no Spanners Dr Gillian Mellville/Mens Health Forum 2009

34 Hamell Communications Own Research

35 Emily A. Ferenczi, Perviz Asaria, Alun D. Hughes, Nishi Chaturvedi MDa and Darrel P. Francis. Their article "Can a Statin Neutralize the Cardiovascular Risk of Unhealthy Dietary Choices?" American Journal of Cardiology Volume 106, Issue 4, 15 August 2010, P 587–592

36 http://webarchive.nationalarchives.gov.uk/+/www.dh.gov.uk/ab/SCOTH/index.htm

37 http://webarchive.nationalarchives.gov.uk/+/www.dh.gov.uk/en/ Publicationsandstatistics/Publications/PublicationsPolicyAndGuidance/DH_4006684

OTHER USEFUL REFERENCES

UK

- Council Directive 2001/83/EC as amended by Directive 2004/27/EC.

- The Medicines Act 1968.

- The Prescription Only Medicines (Human Use) Order 1997 (The POM Order).

- The Medicines (Products other than Veterinary Drugs) (General Sale List) Order 1984 (the GSL Order) .

- The Medicines (Pharmacy and General Sale – Exemption) Order.

- The Medicines (Sale or Supply) (Miscellaneous Provisions) Regulations.

- Marketing Authorisation Regulations.

- Fees Regulations.

EU

A GUIDELINE ON CHANGING THE CLASSIFICATION FOR THE SUPPLY OF A MEDICINAL PRODUCT FOR HUMAN USE (http://ec.europa.eu/health/files/eudralex/vol-2/c/ switchguide_160106_en.pdf)

VOLUME 9A of The Rules Governing Medicinal Products

ec.europa.eu/health/files/eudralex/vol-9/pdf/vol9a_09-2008_en.pdf

EU RMP Template

http://eudravigilance.ema.europa.eu/human/docs/19263206en.pdf

About the Author

Anna Maxwell is a pharmacist with over 25 years' experience of marketing medicines for self medication. She is an entrepreneur, innovator and visionary.

Anna Maxwell

Anna has worked in senior marketing roles for companies such as Boots, Nelsons, Pfizer and Boehringer Ingelheim. Her experience is unique as Anna has worked on 'both sides of the fence': as a pharmacist, a store manager, retail buyer, and as a brand owner in the pharmaceutical arena. Her skills are a dynamic fusion of intuition, practical, hands-on experience and cutting-edge marketing. She is fascinated by consumer behaviour.

Anna studied Pharmacy at Chelsea (Kings College, London) and during her career Anna has overseen some of most ambitious groundbreaking innovation projects from scratch. These include the introduction of the award winning Clikpak for Nelsons and the POM to P switch of tamsulosin (Flomax Relief) for Boehringer Ingelheim.

Anna currently runs a consultancy that specialises in helping pharmaceutical companies convert prescription medicines into non-prescription versions. Her clients have included Top 10 pharmaceutical companies as well as smaller pioneering organisations.

She is an active member of the Self Care Forum.

Acknowledgements

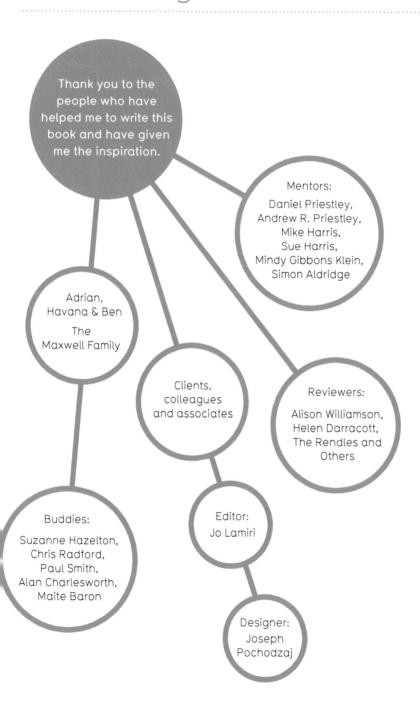

Thank you to the people who have helped me to write this book and have given me the inspiration.

Mentors:
Daniel Priestley,
Andrew R. Priestley,
Mike Harris,
Sue Harris,
Mindy Gibbons Klein,
Simon Aldridge

Adrian,
Havana & Ben

The
Maxwell Family

Clients,
colleagues
and associates

Reviewers:
Alison Williamson,
Helen Darracott,
The Rendles and
Others

Buddies:
Suzanne Hazelton,
Chris Radford,
Paul Smith,
Alan Charlesworth,
Maite Baron

Editor:
Jo Lamiri

Designer:
Joseph
Pochodzaj

Simon Hackett - Director, Pegasus PR

"The rise of self care is one of the defining health trends of this generation, with POM-to-P switches giving pharma companies a leading role and opportunity to unlock value from their portfolios.

Anna's book provides vital insight, strategic guidance and practical advice making it a 'must read' for any business or marketeer considering or involved in a switch."

John D'Arcy - Managing Director, Numark Ltd.

"This book is a must for anyone with an interest in medicine deregulation. Switching is a complex area. This book breaks down the components of the switch process and sets out the "dos and don'ts" in a clear and easily digestible manner."

Sarah Matthew - Chief Executive, Virgo

"An invaluable and long-needed resource for any organisations considering switch opportunities. The consolidated knowledge and experience captured within the book should put an end to the ground hog day effect which is borne out of each and every new switch project attempting to piece together facts and lessons learned about what has gone before. It contains the building blocks for successful switch projects."

Rob Darracott - Chief Executive, Pharmacy Voice

"Switch Dynamics pinpoints the crucial part pharmacists can play in the commercial success of a switch product, from early involvement in the development of a switch product, to advocates and trusted advisers to a public seeking solutions to their health concerns. Pharmacists who want to know more can follow the switch process from assessment of potential molecules to launch, with handy checklists, diagrams and worked examples complementing an insightful text that shines a light on the wider issues that impact successful switch."

Noel Wicks – CEO, Right Medicine Pharmacy

"I've helped with a number of switches over the years and have frequently come across the problems and issues described in Switch Dynamics. I'm quite sure that had the switch teams had access to this book in the early stages of the process their switch would have been better as a result."

Fawz Farhan - Founder, Director, Mediapharm

"I had a quick read and it's really good! I like its stripped down approach using lay language. Switch Dynamics is very readable, and the design and layout is refreshing and memorable."

Matthew Caldwell-Nichols - CEO Precision Marketing Group

"Switch Dynamics has the checklist to help brand owners navigate their switch to become a commercial success. It contains valuable information that can enable them help consumers self care through successful switches."

Contact Details

For more information about switch projects and how I can enhance your switch project , the website is :

www.dynamicswitch.co.uk

To order more copies of Switch Dynamics for your colleagues visit:

www.switchdynamics.co.uk

Join Switchgang on Linked In and keep up to date on the latest switch news

linkedin.com/groups/SwitchGang-4547098

Find me on Twitter:

https://twitter.com/amannamaxwell

See more about my professional credentials on Linked In:

uk.linkedin.com/in/annamaxwell

Contact me for a no obligation discussion contact me by email at:

anna@dynamicswitch.co.uk